Placed People

PLACED PEOPLE

ROOTEDNESS IN G. K. CHESTERTON,
C. S. LEWIS, AND WENDELL BERRY

David Harden

PICKWICK *Publications* · Eugene, Oregon

PLACED PEOPLE
Rootedness in G. K. Chesterton, C. S. Lewis, and Wendell Berry

Copyright © 2015 David Harden. All rights reserved. Except for brief quotations in critical publications or reviews, no part of this book may be reproduced in any manner without prior written permission from the publisher. Write: Permissions, Wipf and Stock Publishers, 199 W. 8th Ave., Suite 3, Eugene, OR 97401.

Pickwick Publications
An Imprint of Wipf and Stock Publishers
199 W. 8th Ave., Suite 3
Eugene, OR 97401

www.wipfandstock.com

ISBN: 978-1-4982-0670-9

Cataloging-in-Publication data:

Harden, David.

    Placed people : rootedness in G. K. Chesterton, C. S. Lewis, and Wendell Berry / David Harden.

    x + 146 p.; 23 cm—Includes bibliographical references and index.

    ISBN: 978-1-4982-0670-9

    1. Chesterton, G. K. (Gilbert Keith), 1874–1936. 2. Lewis, C. S. (Clive Staples), 1898–1963. 3. Berry, Wendell, 1934–. 4. I. Title.

BX1752 H25 2015

Manufactured in the U.S.A.

"Tragic Error" by Denise Levertov, from EVENING TRAIN, copyright © 1992 by Denise Levertov. Reprinted by permission of New Directions Publishing Corp.

Excerpt from "Little Gidding" from FOUR QUARTETS by T.S. Eliot. Copyright 1942 by T.S. Eliot; Copyright © renewed 1970 by Esme Valerie Eliot. Reprinted by permission of Houghton Mifflin Harcourt Publishing Company. Faber & Faber Ltd. All rights reserved.

Excerpts from "The Peace of Wild Things" and "The Gift of Gravity" by Wendell Berry. Copyright © 2012 by Wendell Berry, from NEW COLLECTED POEMS. Reprinted by permission of Counterpoint.

For Melissa and Samuel

ACKNOWLEDGMENTS

This monograph is a lightly edited version of my dissertation for my PhD in English Literature at Marquette University in 2013. Obviously, a project of this magnitude required a lot of assistance, for which I am very grateful. I therefore want to offer my warmest thanks to many generous people who both directly and indirectly helped me along the way.

First, I would like to thank my dissertation director, Dr. Ed Block, for his patience, insight, and encouragement throughout the entire process. I am especially grateful that he graciously sacrificed leisure time in his first year of retirement to help me see this project through. I am not only a better scholar but also a better person because of our many meetings and correspondences together. Whenever I felt overwhelmed during the process of writing, he always offered to me the kind words of encouragement I needed to press on.

I would also like to thank my other committee members, Drs. John Su and Amelia Zurcher, for their questions, suggestions, and insights that have helped me craft a more rigorous, clear, and thoughtful argument. Throughout the writing process they were equal parts supportive and critical. I could not have asked for a better committee.

I am thankful as well for Drs. Deborah Core, Susan Kroeg, and Salome Nnoromele at Eastern Kentucky University and Drs. Devin Brown, Chuck Gobin, Daniel Strait, and Paul Vincent at Asbury University whose teaching and inspiration helped me to reach this milestone.

In addition, I am grateful for the prayerful support and encouragement that my parents, Myron and Diana, and my brother, Wayne, have given me over the years as I have pursued this goal. Though they would

ACKNOWLEDGMENTS

never admit it, there were probably times that they wondered if I would ever finish, and I am thankful that they supported me nevertheless.

Thanks are due to many friends as well, including Jim and Robyn Vining and fellow academics Thomas Bridges and Xan Bozzo. Their encouragement and intellectual discussions throughout my time at Marquette have been indispensable. I am also grateful to the many other friends in Wisconsin and Kentucky who have supported me over the years.

Of course, I must also give a great big thank you to my wife, Melissa, for her patience, support, and encouragement throughout the dissertation process. More than anyone, she knows how difficult the writing process was for me at times and I appreciate her cheerleading during those moments. Above all, I am grateful for her love.

I am very appreciative of all of those at Wipf and Stock Publishers for this opportunity and for their assistance, especially Matthew Wimer and Dr. K. C. Hanson.

Finally, I am eternally grateful to God the Father, God the Son, and God the Holy Spirit, without whose Grace none of what follows would have been possible.

CONTENTS

Acknowledgments vii

Introduction 1

1 Homecoming and Place 11

2 Ethics, Economics, and Place 46

3 Imperialism as Antithesis to Place 72

4 Wholeness, the Humanities, and Place 99

Conclusion 127

Bibliography 135

Name/Subject Index 141

Scripture Index 145

INTRODUCTION

As many others have pointed out, there is much confusion about the purpose of humans in the (post)modern world in which we live. Advertisers tell us we are consumers. Politicians often tell us the same thing: better consumers create a better economy. Clergy tell us we are souls whose purpose is to be saved. Lawyers tell us we are individuals with rights who deserve big settlements when we have been wronged. Environmentalists tell us we are part of a larger community and need to downplay our specio-centrism. Hollywood, ESPN, and other media outlets tell us our purpose is to be consumers of entertainment. The Pentagon, NRA, gun-control advocates, and security companies all tell us our purpose is to keep ourselves, our loved-ones, and possessions safe, though by markedly different means. With all of these competing and often contradictory messages, the question remains unanswered: "What are people for?"

Classically, humans were considered to have a *telos* towards which to order their lives. Their *telos* was some purpose reserved especially for humans that was distinct from the *teloi* of animals and nature. According to Aristotle, understanding their *telos* was essential for humans in order for them to live a "good life." In other words, knowing the purpose of humans was essential to defining the "goods" required to achieve this purpose. According to Charles Taylor, Aristotle distinguished two levels of a "good life." The essential level shared by all is what Taylor calls the "ordinary life" concerned with the day-to-day needs for shelter, food, and other family provisions.[1] After this base level of the "good life" is achieved, humans can then pursue the higher goods of contemplation and politics.[2]

---

1. Taylor, *Sources of the Self*, 211.
2. Ibid., 212.

However, Taylor says, Aristotle's prioritizing was reversed in the Reformation and Enlightenment and so for moderns[3] the "ordinary life" is privileged over contemplation and politics. As a result, two important shifts took place. First, the church (which borrowed from Aristotle) was rejected in favor of the individual.[4] Second, the "instrumental stance" was made "central."[5] This "transform[ed] the understanding of the cosmos from an order of signs or Forms, whose unity lies in their relation to a meaningful whole, into an order of things producing reciprocal effects in each other, whose unity in God's plan must be that of interlocking purposes."[6] This change in perception opened the door for individuals to engage the world and each other instrumentally, as they sought to define and achieve "ordinary life" as the highest good.

Rejecting a shared belief in an over-arching cosmic order, modern humans are left to make sense of the "goods" left to them from the old order. For Taylor, this makes such individualistic "frameworks" "inescapable" and "problematic."[7] He states, "What is common to them all is the sense that no framework is shared by everyone, can be taken for granted as *the* framework tout court, can sink to the phenomenological status of unquestioned fact."[8] These problematic frameworks create three types of people for Taylor: those who "self-conscious[ly]" accept a traditional position, those who accept their framework while "pluralist[ically]" allowing others to hold different frameworks, and those who "are aware of their own uncertainties" and are "seeking."[9] Borrowing Alasdair MacIntyre's term, Taylor says of this third type that they are on a "quest."[10]

Many moderns fall into this third category. This third group of modern individuals, influenced by the culture of the late nineteenth and early twentieth century, might also be seen as including within it the cultural sub-group called the High Modernists (people like Eliot, Pound, Fitzgerald,

---

3. I use this term broadly to mean what Taylor means, signaling a fundamental shift in the way post-Enlightenment humans view themselves as individuals each possessing a "self" distinct and divorced from their environment.

4. Taylor, *Sources of the Self*, 216.

5. Ibid., 233.

6. Ibid.

7. Ibid., 17.

8. Ibid.

9. Ibid. Perhaps British rock band The Who best summed up this ethical dilemma of modern culture in their 1970 single "The Seeker."

10. Ibid.

INTRODUCTION

and Woolf, hereafter referred to as modernists). Modernists primarily consist of the rapidly disappearing high culture within the larger group of the modern everyday population. The modern everyday population, post-Reformation, had demolished the old hierarchical public order that placed politics and contemplation (public life) as the highest form of the good life, privileging the ordinary life (private life) instead.[11] As a result, says Taylor:

> Virtually nothing in the domain of mythology, metaphysics, or theology stands in this fashion as publicly available background today. But that doesn't mean that there is nothing in any of those domains that [High Modern] poets may not want to reach out to in order to say what they want to say, no moral sources they descry there that they want to open for us. What it does mean is that their opening these domains, in default of being a move against a firm background, is an articulation of personal vision.[12]

Therefore, people in the modern age have dealt with these issues of human purpose by setting out on quests of discovery, rejecting and leaving the traditions and orthodoxies they inherited in order to forge for themselves a "new" identity. In their quest they often lived mobile or transient lives, divorced from a community and personal vision. At its most extreme, perhaps, is the desire held by some moderns to escape the Earth completely, famously discussed by Hannah Arendt[13] and explored extensively in science fiction from *War of the Worlds* to *Battlestar Galactica*. Less extreme, perhaps, was the desire in modernist literature for a new form to reflect a new framework. For example, F. Scott Fitzgerald sought for "something really NEW in form, idea, structure—the model for the age that Joyce and Stein are searching for, that Conrad didn't find."[14] Likewise, Woolf sought a "voyage out," away from stultifying traditions and orthodoxies. As a result, many modernists on this risky quest physically rejected institutions and nations, becoming expatriates like Joyce and Hemingway.

Likewise, many modern Christians embrace a "tradition" of longing for heaven as an escape from this world. Basing their beliefs on the passages

---

11. See Arendt, *The Human Condition* and Taylor, *Sources of the Self*, chapter 13, "'God Loveth Adverbs.'"

12. Taylor, *Sources of the Self*, 491–92.

13. Arendt, *Human Condition*, 1. Arendt writes: "In 1957, an earth-born object made by man was launched into the universe . . . The immediate reaction . . . was relief about the first 'step toward escape from men's imprisonment to the earth.'"

14. Fitzgerald, "Letter to Max Perkins, May 1, 1925," 47.

3

in the Bible that describe Christians as strangers and aliens on earth, they limit their theology by making heaven the real "home" for humans—an other and outer place. This tradition has many of its roots in the post-Enlightenment era, arguably from the same foundations used by moderns longing to escape the problems of life here on earth. In fact, one way post-Enlightenment Christians distance themselves from earthly problems is to avoid community with other Christians. This theology of escape and individualism (i.e., a spiritual "personal vision") ignores scripture that also talks about a new earth—a redeemed, restored earth—as well as places emphasis on community. Recently, Christian authors such as Randy Alcorn and N. T. Wright have sought to restore a holistic view of heaven to popular Christian theology.

Of course, there were also modernists who, embarking on "quests" of their own, re-discovered their inherited traditions and, in accepting them, chose to set down roots in a place. For example, T. S. Eliot said in the fourth section of *Four Quartets*, titled *Little Gidding*:

> We shall not cease from exploration
> And the end of all our exploring
> Will be to arrive where we started
> And to know the place for the first time.[15]

Eliot is here reflecting as an older poet who, after all of the explorations in his early poetry, found his place in orthodox traditions of the past. Eliot is not alone in his rejection of youthful modernism for a return to orthodox tradition. Three other such authors are G. K. Chesterton, C. S. Lewis, and Wendell Berry.

Chesterton, Lewis, and Berry are key literary figures both because of the relationship of their ideas to each other and for the breadth of their writings, stretching from the turn of the twentieth century to this day. Chesterton, perhaps best known for his Father Brown stories, would have considered himself first a journalist. He published prolifically from the turn of the century until his death in 1936. He wrote essays, poems, short stories, novels, biographies, and even a successful play. Besides writing, he is also well-known for his spirited debates with H. G. Wells and George Bernard Shaw. Unlike Chesterton, Lewis was a "scholar" in the traditional sense, earning three firsts at Oxford, then tutored and taught as a fellow for three decades at Magdalen College, Oxford before becoming Professor of

---

15. Eliot, *Collected Poems: 1909–1962*, 208.

INTRODUCTION

Medieval and Renaissance English at Cambridge near the end of his life. After publishing a couple of unsuccessful volumes of poetry, he switched to prose, writing both fiction and essays. He is perhaps best known for his series of BBC talks about Christianity during the Second World War (later published as *Mere Christianity*) and for his *Chronicles of Narnia* stories. Both Chesterton and Lewis are also known for their volumes of apologetics, which they wrote throughout their careers. For Lewis, the religious nature of these essays and talks cost him professionally, when he was passed over for a professorship at Oxford. Though Chesterton and Lewis both wrote Christian apologetics, the traditions to which they converted in adulthood and from which they wrote out of differed: Chesterton became Roman Catholic and Lewis became Anglican.

Though to some it may seem odd to include Berry with possibly the two central Christian apologists of the twentieth century, I believe that Berry is rooted in orthodox Christianity and that the disparaging statements he has made about Christianity have been about the corrupted institution, not about biblical tenets. He, like Lewis and Chesterton before him, is a prophetic voice calling for Christians and non-Christians alike to return home. Many others, both Protestant and Catholic, have acknowledged this resistance Berry has towards institutionalized Christianity, while still embracing him as an orthodox Christian. Allan Carlson, for example, acknowledges that Berry has "been iconoclastic toward organized Christianity," especially regarding "the dualism of orthodox Christian eschatology—setting this world off against the next—[that] has been the source of agricultural and environmental crises."[16] Nevertheless, Carlson also acknowledges that Berry's solution is "derived from the Kingdom of God."[17] Even more forcefully, P. Travis Kroeker states, "Wendell Berry's prophetic cultural criticism is rooted in a sacramental imagination."[18] Kroeker continues:

> It may ring strange to call Berry's imagination "sacramental," since he is neither a Catholic like Flannery O'Connor (in whose writing explicitly sacramental symbolism is in prominent display) nor, indeed, very overtly "religious" at all. I expect that Berry would strongly resist any attempt to locate him religiously, or perhaps identify him as a "religious" or "Christian" writer. In these regards perhaps Berry is typically liberal Protestant—deeply suspicious of

---

16. Carlson, "Wendell Berry," 100.
17. Ibid., 101.
18. Kroeker, "Sexuality," 120.

institutional Christianity, especially its claims to authority, and of the separation between the sacred and the secular . . . in everyday life.[19]

As evidence, Kroeker refers to Berry's disparaging comments in *The Long-Legged House*, explored below in chapter 1, and also to Berry's interview with Katherine Dalton, discussed below. Nevertheless, after this lengthy qualifier Kroeker still places Berry squarely in the Christian tradition, asserting: "In this essay I shall nevertheless attempt to 'claim' his work for membership in the Christian community—not in an ideological, triumphalist form (whether Protestant or Catholic, liberal or conservative) but in the form that bears witness to the messianic or Christic mystery that would restore all creation to its intended ordering of love in God."[20] In a sense, then, we see a hesitation by members in the academic community to define the religious aspect that pervades Berry's writing.

This hesitation has not gone unnoticed. In a review of the collection within which Carlson's and Kroeker's essays appear, *Wendell Berry: Life and Work*, Robert Benson is astute to point out the elephant in the room, hesitantly stepped around by most of the authors in the collection: the role of religion in Berry's writings. Benson states:

> The question of the importance of religion in Berry's work remains vexed, and neither Berry nor the contributors to this volume have been precisely helpful . . . Though reluctant in some way to deal with it directly and occasionally confused by it, many of the essayists in this collection call attention to the strong religious element in Berry's work. Reluctance and confusion are sometimes the result of the metaphysical uncertainty of some of the contributors, but Berry himself is not entirely settled in his convictions, and his take on Christianity is hard to pin down.[21]

He even specifically mentions Carlson and Kroeker, saying of their religious language, for example: "The word *orthodox* is certainly misleading in this context and can only be taken to refer to a certain brand of American Protestantism, and a phrase such as 'sacramental imagination' loses meaning in the context of liberal Protestantism."[22] Referring to Catholic authors like Chesterton, Sayers, and other Distributists, Benson shows how

19. Ibid.
20. Ibid.
21. Benson, "Curing Babylon," 279.
22. Ibid.

Berry's religious views align themselves with true orthodox Christianity. He concludes: "It is plain that, from the precise and explicit biblical matter in such collections as *Watch with Me* to the vision of Heaven at the end of *A World Lost*, Berry's fiction takes the religious life of Port William seriously; and in his political and social commentary Berry again and again holds up the imitation of Christ as the standard against which we measure our political and moral judgments."[23] In sum, Benson sees Berry's writing in "fundamental agreement with Catholic social teaching."[24]

In this view, Benson is not alone. The Catholic journal *Communio* recently featured a special issue on the topic of money that included a reprinted essay by Berry and two essays that explore Berry's economic thought. According to Mark Shiffman, "[W]e find in Berry, as in Aristotle, a vision of the profound intertwining of the first two parts of practical philosophy (Ethics and Œconomics)."[25] In the other essay on Berry, Nathan Schlueter draws connections between Berry's novel *Remembering* and John Paul II's *The Theology of the Body*.[26] Of course, while Berry's writings are not intentionally or overtly Catholic, that such orthodox Catholic thinkers as those in *Communio* do take seriously his thoughts on such issues as economics and sexuality is intriguing and speaks to the importance Berry places on religion, specifically Christianity.

Certainly, Chesterton, Lewis, and Berry share views that suggest a common conception of orthodoxy that acts as the foundation on which they build their similar-but-distinct worldviews. In order to define what I mean by "orthodoxy," I will begin with the definition Chesterton offers in his book of the same title. Chesterton prefaces his book by stating: "These essays are concerned only to discuss the actual fact that the central Christian theology (sufficiently summarized in the Apostles' Creed) is the best root of energy and sound ethics. They are not intended to discuss the very fascinating but quite different question of what is the present seat of authority for the proclamation of that creed . . ."[27] Here we see Chesterton defining orthodoxy by emphasizing the beliefs held in the Apostle's Creed,

---

23. Ibid., 280.

24. Ibid., 281.

25. Shiffman, "An Ethic," 493. The third part is Politics, which Shiffman claims Berry neglects "except to the extent that he identifies the causal role of public policies in the destruction of the productive household."

26. Schlueter, "Healing the Hidden Wound."

27. Chesterton, *Orthodoxy*, 7.

while dismissing any specific institutional particulars that he himself may have at the time believed. Even Berry, who is so critical of institutionalized Christianity, upholds the pre-institutional credal elements of a Creator, Creation, and the importance of looking to Christ as a model for living. Nevertheless, when many critics discuss Berry's religious beliefs, his critique of Gnosticism in contemporary Christianity tends to dominate their discussion. Yes, Berry does seriously believe we are in peril if we accept a dualism that separates body and spirit. However, we must keep separate this modern version of Western Christianity from the comparable forms of orthodox Christianity that Chesterton, Lewis, and Berry emphasize. Once again, Benson is useful. He states, "Traditional Christianity has been naming and condemning the dualist heresy in all its forms for centuries."[28] In all of his condemnations, then, Berry is recovering an orthodoxy that precedes the dualism born out of the Enlightenment and the Industrial Revolution.

For sure, Berry's writings align well with Chesterton's definition of orthodoxy, because they again and again give Christian theology central importance in discussions of ethics, while at the same time remaining neutral toward any specific Christian institution.[29] One could argue that Berry's disdain for institutions is a natural by-product of his 1960s early adulthood. This is where Berry parts ways with Chesterton and Lewis. Though all three see many of the same problems, Chesterton and Lewis have found a place within institutions of the church to voice their critiques. Berry, perhaps ironically, emphasizes the importance of place and community in his worldview and yet also largely rejects institutionalized forms of community. He makes no claims to regular church attendance, and his Sabbath poems involve his personal reflections that stem from Sabbath walks in nature. In other words, he chooses to participate in some communities, like those of nature and neighbor, while distrusting others, like Protestant denominations that appoint non-community members as pastors of rural churches. However, adherence to institutions is not absolutely necessary for orthodoxy. Rather, adherence to a common doctrine (tradition) by a community is the essence of orthodoxy. One cannot be orthodox to himself or

---

28. Benson, "Curing Babylon," 279.

29. Orthodoxy, with a lowercase "o," is the right term to describe Berry because he shares with Chesterton and Lewis the Judeo-Christian tradition and many specific social practices. He is not "Orthodox" (situated in specific affiliation like Roman Catholicism or Anglicanism) but is "orthodox" (conforming to the traditionally accepted Judeo-Christian beliefs and practices). Therefore, I am claiming that all three authors share "orthodoxy," not "Orthodoxy."

herself, but rather only in relationship to someone else (who is by definition not orthodox). Therefore, orthodoxy is something only a community can do. It is the comparable orthodox vision these authors articulate in their writings, regardless of their particular institutional practice, that have important implications for our own understanding of our fragmented modern worldviews. Taken together, these authors show Christians confronting the identity crisis of modern humans, described above in the opening paragraph.

What do Chesterton, Lewis, and Berry offer as an alternative? In other words, how do they confront the assumptions of our modern technological and science-as-religion culture? First, they place an emphasis on returning home, both spiritually and physically. The authors demonstrate this both in their own lives and in their writings. Second, they emphasize the important connection between place and ethics. At its roots, this connection is about economics. The *Oxford English Dictionary* defines "economy" as "[t]he way in which something is managed; the management of resources; household management." From the Classical period to Middle Ages, the word meant "[t]he proper management of the body; (also) the rules which control a person's mode of living; regimen, diet" as well as "[a] household; a society or other structure ordered after the manner of a family," and it is telling that after science ushered in industrialism "economy" is now almost exclusively used to discuss money.[30] Chesterton, Lewis, and Berry would have us return to the original meaning of the word. Third, they emphasized the importance of contentment with boundaries, arising from the self-limiting aspect of choosing to be rooted in place. This contentment allows us to respect others, including other humans, communities, and the natural world, and it allows us to reject all forms of imperialism. Fourth, they emphasize that liberal education (and especially the humanities) plays a crucial role in helping us integrate the previous three things and they warn against the dangers of "specialization."

Their returns to Christianity plunged them deeper into the life of this world and its traditions and problems. In other words, while many secular and Christian moderns alike sought to escape the Earth and its problems, these authors chose to go back to a pre-modern, or at least pre-Enlightenment Christian tradition that sent them deeper into the Earth, giving them a new way to see and interact with all that surrounded them.

30. *Oxford English Dictionary*, 3rd ed., s.v. "economy."

Each one's re-discovery of a comparable conception of orthodox Christianity provided a new imaginative perspective with which to view the world. They saw the world with a sacramental imagination. That is, everything they saw in the world around them was connected in their imaginations to a larger cosmos ordered toward a supreme being. This sacramental imagination helped them view the world in a much less utilitarian way, setting them apart and opposed to many modernist elites who instrumentally use people, places, and the natural world.

Chesterton, Lewis, and Berry write against the modern age, returning to a set of beliefs derived from orthodox religion, and accepting limits within a largely Judeo-Christian context. In doing so, they critique the scientific, technological milieu that sought (and seeks) to escape such limits. Examining how Chesterton, Lewis, and Berry confront the increasingly commercial, materialist, utilitarian, ends-justify-the-means culture of the twentieth and twenty-first centuries will help underscore the relevance of such literature to our current culture. Perhaps most of all, we need to include in our understanding of the humanities these authors' insights into the importance that place, community, and orthodoxy hold in ethics. Their insights function as a crucial balance to our all-too-common tendency towards individualism and utilitarianism in our modern age. Studying these authors' writings, therefore, allows us to understand and envision the contemporary relevance of the countercultural values that they propound.

1

HOMECOMING AND PLACE

Departures and Returns in the Lives of Chesterton, Lewis, and Berry

CHESTERTON, LEWIS, AND BERRY all experienced major returns in their lives, returns to roots and limits. "Return" refers to the way in which all three authors were born into families that were culturally Judeo-Christian, were then challenged as young adults by modern narratives of limitless progress to reject this tradition, but finally chose to reject these modern narratives in favor of something resembling a rooted orthodox Judeo-Christian worldview and the limits that go with it. These returns were brought about in ways unique to the authors, but one major commonality among them is that the returns happened when they discovered and chose to embrace an idea of "the Good" that transcended the merely material. Charles Taylor calls "higher-order goods of this kind 'hypergoods', i.e., goods which not only are incomparably more important than others but provide the standpoint from which these must be weighed, judged, [and] decided about."[1] These "hypergoods" are the ideals that contribute to the wholeness of a place, including those who dwell in it. This concept of "wholeness" derives from the Judeo-Christian account of creation in Genesis—everything God created was deemed good and existed within an assigned place, but humanity rejected this order and thus broke apart the original "wholeness."

---

1. Taylor, *Sources of the Self*, 63.

Therefore, the Judeo-Christian teleology includes consideration of an eventual restoration and return.[2] These "goods" led these authors to various homecomings, categorized loosely as spiritual and physical. For Chesterton and Lewis, discovering and accepting a return to Christian beliefs helped lead them to an imaginative perspective rooted in place. For Berry, discovering and accepting his vocation as a placed farmer/writer led him physically back home to Kentucky early in his career where he was able to ask religious questions about place that allowed him to wrestle with his inherited Baptist faith.

As a young man, Chesterton rejected his religious cultural roots and set out on a journey to discover some new philosophy as a replacement. He, like many others at the turn of the twentieth century in England, was hoping to escape the stultifying Victorian values and the version of Christian religion that went with them. However, in setting out on a journey of discovery or progress, Chesterton ironically realized when he finished that he had actually returned past his Victorian upbringing and rediscovered orthodox Christianity. As he puts it in *Orthodoxy*, "I did try to found a heresy of my own; and when I had put the last touches to it, I discovered that it was orthodoxy."[3]

What seeds of orthodoxy were planted in Chesterton's childhood that made escape impossible when he tried to found, or discover, his heresy? Briefly, Gilbert Keith Chesterton was born on 29 May 1874 to Edward and Marie Chesterton. Chesterton's parents were bohemian types[4] who, as good

---

2. Though even a post-structuralist like Jacques Derrida may consider the issue of totality, most postmodern writers are suspicious of what they would call meta-narratives that enforce a false sense of wholeness or closure. I am arguing, following Taylor, that these meta-narratives are really "inescapable frameworks," even for postmoderns. See *Sources of the Self*, chapter 1. Near the end of *Sources of the Self*, Taylor states: "For Derrida there is nothing but deconstruction, which swallows up the old hierarchical distinctions between philosophy and literature, and between men and women, but just as readily could swallow up equal/unequal, community/disorder, uncoerced/constrained dialogue, and the like. Nothing emerges from this flux worth affirming, and so what in fact comes to be celebrated is the deconstructing power itself... pure untrammeled freedom" (489). He continues, "The very claim not to be oriented by a notion of the good... reflects that the underlying ideal is some variant of that most invisible, because it is the most pervasive, of all modern goods, unconstrained freedom" (489). Finally, he states, "To the extent that this kind of freedom is held up as the essence of 'post-modernity', as it is by Jean-François Lyotard, it shows this to be a prolongation of the least impressive side of modernism" (489).

3. Chesterton, *Orthodoxy*, 6.

4. Oddie, *Chesterton*, 18.

Victorians, retained the Christian virtues while dismissing the Christian creed.[5] Mocking modern psychology, he says in his *Autobiography*: "I regret that I have no gloomy and savage father to offer to the public gaze as the true cause of all my tragic heritage; no pale-faced and partially poisoned mother whose suicidal instincts have cursed me with the temptations of the artistic temperament . . . And I am compelled to confess that I look back to that landscape of my first days with a pleasure that should doubtless be reserved for the Utopias of the Futurist."[6]

One of his earliest and most influential memories was of a toy theater his father built for him, which helped instill in him a love for limits: "Apart from the fact of it [the toy theater] being my first memory, I have several reasons for putting it first . . . All my life I have loved edges; and the boundary-line that brings one thing sharply against another. All my life I have loved frames and limits; and I will maintain that the largest wilderness looks larger seen through a window."[7] In chapter 4 I will address the issue of limits. Summing up his childhood, Chesterton states, "In a word; I have never lost the sense that this was my real life; the real beginning of what should have been a more real life; a lost experience in the land of the living."[8] He would have to journey through a period of psychological and spiritual hell in his adolescence and young adulthood before he "discovered" that his love for limits had helped him rediscover orthodoxy. This is not unlike the mission of the humanities, for which rediscovery is as important as discovery is to the sciences—a necessary task.

Chesterton refers to his adolescence as "the period of youth which is full of doubts and morbidities and temptations; and which, though in my case mainly subjective, has left in my mind for ever a certitude upon the objective solidity of Sin."[9] He further states, "I am not proud of believing in the Devil. To put it more correctly, I am not proud of knowing the Devil. I made his acquaintance by my own fault; and followed it up along lines which, had they been followed further, might have led me to devil-worship or the devil knows what."[10] This period is 1892 to 1894, during which Chesterton took a year off after finishing at St. Paul's public school

---

5. Ward, *Gilbert*, 6.
6. Chesterton, *Autobiography*, 38.
7. Ibid., 41.
8. Ibid., 59.
9. Ibid., 87.
10. Ibid., 88.

and then attended the Slade School of Art at University College, London.[11] It was during this period that Chesterton dabbled in spiritualism, even using an Ouija board with his younger brother Cecil. He also learned about modern art at the Slade School, especially the then-popular Impressionism. His dislike of Impressionism (remember, he always loved "edges") and the prevailing mood of pessimism he encountered during this period produced real internal turmoil.

This prevailing mood of pessimism primarily, for Chesterton, stemmed from Walter Pater's "art for art's sake" and his influence on a major emblem of the early 1890s, Oscar Wilde.[12] Chesterton viewed this philosophy's not-too-subtle motive to do away with morality and any external good to focus on immediate pleasure as a nightmare, because of the pessimistic mood that inevitably accompanied it. For Chesterton, Pater's regard for temporal pleasure as the aim of art only leads to a never-ending pursuit of greater and greater pleasures—it is a pursuit that cannot be fulfilled, leading to despair, even of life itself.[13] This despair of life was the ultimate evil of the *fin de siècle* for Chesterton. Disgusted, Chesterton fought against it:

> But I was still thinking the thing out by myself, with little help from philosophy and no real help from religion, I invented a rudimentary and makeshift mystical theory of my own. It was substantially this; that even mere existence, reduced to its most primary limits, was extraordinary enough to be exciting. Anything was magnificent as compared with nothing. Even if the very daylight were a dream, it was a day-dream; it was not a nightmare.[14]

Chesterton emerged from this period as an optimist, and his life's work from this point on can be viewed as a battle against the pessimism of the *fin de siècle*.[15]

This philosophy concerning optimism perhaps is best demonstrated in Chesterton's companion works *Heretics* (1905) and *Orthodoxy* (1908). *Heretics* is loosely structured around many chapters that individually

---

11. See Oddie, *Chesterton*, who clears up inaccuracies in previous biographers' timelines.

12. Ibid., 108–10.

13. To be fair, Pater was also after "dignity" and worth, but Chesterton does not discuss these aims. Perhaps Chesterton feels they are lost in the public outworking of Pater's philosophy of art in the lives of its adherents.

14. Chesterton, *Autobiography*, 98.

15. Oddie states, "His hostility toward 'the Pessimists' . . . continued to define his own literary identity," *Chesterton*, 375.

address writers whom Chesterton deems heretics, thinkers of his time such as Rudyard Kipling, H. G. Wells, G. B. Shaw, and George Moore. Chesterton respects these individuals for having a creed (being dogmatic) but believes their ideas are wrong. Due to the nature of his task, Chesterton does not lay out a sustained argument, but various statements throughout can be pieced together to build the framework of his philosophy regarding topics such as ethics, science, progress, and place.

One significant problem in modern ethics, felt Chesterton, was that it had lost or rejected all notions of an ideal, a good, towards which to point.[16] Even if our best efforts to attain "the ethical ideal" are "hopeless," they are still more "wholesome" than "modern morality, on the other hand, [which] can only point with absolute conviction to the horrors that follow breaches of law; its only certainty is a certainty of ill. It can only point to imperfection. It has no perfection to point to."[17] This does not mean that people cannot be good, "[f]or many such are good only through a withering knowledge of evil."[18] This negative moral philosophy had crept into art, especially in modern realism. Chesterton despised this type of writing, saying polemically, "Modern realists are indeed Terrorists, like the dynamiters; and they fail just as much in their effort to create a thrill. Both realists and dynamiters are well-meaning people engaged in the task, so obviously ultimately hopeless, of using science to promote morality."[19] This part about science and morality is important; it helps explain why he was so opposed to privileging science as a replacement for religion. He was rejecting the modernist tendency to leave religion and embrace science as a substitute to derive morality. Chesterton was instead favoring a return to the integrative, ordered, hierarchical world view with its set of values based in Greek and Judeo-Christian tradition provided by orthodox religion as an alternative.

---

16. MacIntyre traces this problem to the failure of the Enlightenment Project. Whereas the classical conception of human nature had three components: "untutored human nature, man-as-he-could-be-if-he-realized-his *telos* and the moral precepts which enable him to pass from one state to the other," the Enlightenment Project rejected "both Protestant and Catholic theology and the scientific and philosophical [aspects of] Aristotelianism." This "eliminate[d] any notion of man-as-he-could-be-if-he-realized-his-*telos*" and "[left] behind a moral scheme composed of two remaining elements whose relationship becomes unclear." *After Virtue*, 54–55.

17. Chesterton, *Heretics*, 9.

18. Ibid., 9.

19. Ibid., 12.

This rejection of religion as source for a world view sums up much of the pessimism of the *fin de siècle*: a philosophy with no positive ideal towards which to strive leaves only "unconstrained freedom" as its goal, leading to destructive lifestyles and a despair about life itself.[20] For example, Shaw once said in praise of Ibsen's morality, "The golden rule is that there is no golden rule."[21] Chesterton strongly disagreed with this statement. Eliminating all positive moral ideals from one's philosophy of life left one vulnerable to committing evil.[22] This is because, Chesterton says, "[the] absence of an enduring positive ideal . . . does leave us face to face with the problem of a human consciousness filled with very definite images of evil, and with no definite image of good."[23] The modern ethical philosophy, then, varied considerably from past ages which, says Chesterton, "have sweated and been crucified in an attempt to realize what is really the right life, what was really the good man."[24] Certainly Aristotle's ethical philosophy sought to achieve this. In contrast, "Every one of the popular modern phrases and ideals is a dodge in order to shirk the problem of what is good."[25]

For Chesterton, therefore, lack of a moral ideal rendered meaningless the popular concept of "progress." Chesterton, taking an Aristotelian perspective, believed that in order to progress there has to be an ideal to progress towards. In his characteristic polemical manner, he states, "Nobody has any business to use the word 'progress' unless he has a definite creed and a cast-iron code of morals. Nobody can be progressive without being doctrinal."[26] However, this does not rule out any possibility of progress: "I do not, therefore, say that the word 'progress' is unmeaning; I say it is unmeaning without the previous definition of a moral doctrine, and that it can only be applied to groups of persons who hold that doctrine in common."[27] Chesterton's moral philosophy at this point again appears

20. Taylor, *Sources of the Self*, 489. See n. 2, above.

21. Ibid., 12.

22. As MacIntyre states, "What is abundantly clear is that in everyday life as in moral philosophy the replacement of Aristotelian or Christian teleology by a definition of the virtues in terms of the passions is not so much or at all the replacement of one set of criteria by another, but rather a movement towards and into a situation where there are no longer any clear criteria." *Sources*, 235–36.

23. Chesterton, *Heretics*, 12–13.

24. Ibid., 13.

25. Ibid.

26. Ibid., 15.

27. Ibid.

similar to Aristotle and our own modern day Aristotelian philosophers such as Alasdair MacIntyre, who hold a communitarian understanding of ethics, which believes ethics should be rooted in a commonly held belief of the ideal or good. An example of this communitarian understanding would be the Amish, who hold the same Judeo-Christian tradition as other communities, but they more narrowly define it. Amish communities are not relativist, because their ideal goes back to a source.

There is a big difference between orienting one's life according to a *telos* and ordering one's life according to a vague idea of "progress." A *telos* presupposes a specific End and therefore a map can be made to help us reach that End. Progress, as the term is popularly used, rejects any traditional understanding of an End, and therefore, whatever maps are created has no way to provide orientation. We need a larger framework and orthodoxy, or a worldview that can be taken as an "unquestioned fact," is a necessary condition for a viable *telos*.[28] In other words, in order for us to have a shared public *telos*, we need to have a common foundational framework. Until we have something like such a shared background to help us shape an ideal, our public selves will likely tend towards the individualistic and we will work at cross-purposes.

Finally, in *Heretics* Chesterton shows how adherence to place makes edges "disappear." What I mean is not that the edges actually disappear, but that we cease to notice them because we are looking inward, rather than outward. In fact, edges can be important because they can focus to stay put and look inward at our place. A great example of this phenomenon is seen in the Disney classic *The Swiss Family Robinson*. Though at first the ocean surrounding the island on which the Robinsons shipwreck seems like a limiting edge, after a while they realize the wealth and beauty of the island and create their own society, a society that we (the audience) find rich and adventurous—thus the appeal.[29] Chesterton had already explained this phenomenon, "The moment we are rooted in a place, the place vanishes. We live like a tree with the whole strength of the universe."[30] What Chesterton means by "place vanishes," is that we no longer see it from the outside, as a separate thing with edges. From the inside, place phenomenologically "disappears." One thing striking about this statement is that it sounds so

---

28. Taylor, *Sources of the Self*, 17.

29. In fact, we almost forget about the ocean until some pirates show up near the end of the movie.

30. Chesterton, *Heretics*, 22.

much like how deep ecologists might talk about the symbiotic relationship between humans and nature, though written more than a century ago. This similarity is no coincidence.

Perhaps the "tree" metaphor resembles environmental language because the ecological worldview takes rootedness in place as Taylor's "unquestioned fact."[31] In other words, the ecological worldview accepts without question a part of the prior orthodoxy—a public framework that used to be common to all. Another striking aspect is that it emphasizes a significant part of Chesterton's philosophical outlook: by using paradox, he has highlighted a simple truth about the way our imaginations perceive space. Only when we stop and view a place from the inside do we see the various things that make up the place—a complete world within a world. In fact, Chesterton states, "The telescope makes the world smaller; it is only the microscope that makes it larger."[32] He therefore views the then new technological invention of the motorcar as a symptom of the modern outlook of his time that privileges motion—progress—rather than appreciating (loving) what is already there. Unfortunately, we miss so much if we do not allow ourselves to become rooted. He states, "It is inspiriting without doubt to whizz in a motorcar round the earth, to feel Arabia as a whirl of sand and China as a flash of rice-fields. But Arabia is not a whirl of sand and China is not a flash of rice-fields. They are ancient civilizations with strange virtues buried like treasures."[33] He continues, "The man standing in his own kitchen-garden, with fairyland opening at the gate, is the man with large ideas. His mind creates distance; the motorcar stupidly destroys it."[34] This image is reminiscent of George MacDonald, one of Chesterton's favorite authors and one of the authors who helped save him from the pessimism of his youth. Finally, Chesterton says: "And [motorcar civilization] watches from its splendid parochialism, possibly with a smile of amusement, . . . going its triumphant way, outstripping time, consuming space, seeing all and seeing nothing, roaring on at last to the capture of the solar system, only to find the sun cockney and the stars suburban."[35]

31. Taylor, *Sources of the Self*, 17.

32. Chesterton, *Heretics*, 23. Here is an example of where Chesterton shows that he is not totally dismissive of all science or technology.

33. Ibid., 23.

34. Ibid.

35. Ibid., 24. Once again, this last statement is reminiscent of Arendt: "The most radical change in the human condition we can imagine would be an emigration of men from the earth to some other planet." *Human Condition*, 10.

For Chesterton, the motorcar was the type of technology that best exemplified the fast-paced lifestyle of modern humans. Obviously, this lifestyle has not slowed down but only become faster as technology has "improved." Our cars have become faster, we now rely on supersonic jets for transportation, and we can even launch humans into space so that they have an outside perspective on the earth, providing us all with an iconic image of earth as an abstract mix of blues, browns, greens, and swirling whites. Of course, this "blue marble" image can be seen as working both for and against an ecological view—a fragile world that must be saved, or used up, or abandoned altogether.[36] This "motorcar civilization" mindset lends itself to important ethical problems. What is fascinating is that Lewis and Berry both make similar negative remarks about this type of modern "motorcar" thinking. We will explore their comments and the ethical issues raised a little later in the chapter.

Chesterton's contemporaries, especially satiric nineties novelist and playwright, G. S. Street, criticized Chesterton for attacking others' philosophies in *Heretics* without laying out his own. In response to this "challenge," Chesterton wrote *Orthodoxy*.[37] In the book's introduction, Chesterton reveals another crucial part of his philosophy of life:

> I have often had a fancy for writing a romance about an English yachtsman who slightly miscalculated his course and discovered England under the impression that it was a new island in the South Seas . . . This at least seems to me the main problem for philosophers, and is in a manner the main problem of this book. *How can we contrive to be at once astonished at the world and yet at home in it?*[38]

What is it about this quote that has allowed it to live on for over a hundred years? The answer lies in a teleologically coherent worldview that allows for the astonishment of homecoming. This astonishment at homecoming is related to the importance of place from *Heretics*. There, place became larger once one set down roots and began to look around. Here, Chesterton is taking this idea a step further: he adds the welcome feeling of "home" to the astonishment at enjoying the newness, or uniqueness of observing one's immediate place. This drama finds its fullest expression in

---

36. Perhaps to populate the moon, as one American presidential primary candidate suggested in 2012.

37. Chesterton, *Orthodoxy*, 1.

38. Ibid., 3, italics mine.

Chesterton's novel *Manalive*, discussed below. As noted earlier, Chesterton connects this parable to his philosophy by declaring, "The man from the yacht thought he was the first to find England; I thought I was the first to find Europe. I did try to found a heresy of my own; and when I had put the last touches to it, I discovered that it was orthodoxy."[39]

Like Chesterton, Lewis also rejected his religious upbringing as an adolescent. As Lewis puts it, "I ceased to be a Christian."[40] This led him on a journey to discover his philosophy of life on his own, like his other contemporaries from 1918 to 1930. He was first an atheist, then an agnostic, before finally becoming "the most dejected and reluctant convert in all England."[41] Just as Chesterton's, Lewis's quest to discover a new framework led him to return to orthodox Christianity, though his journey took him a bit longer. Also, like Chesterton, the roots for his return began in his childhood, especially with regards to a fascination with "joy" and its relationship to place, as we shall see. Lewis sought to build his framework around the concept of "joy," but his quest led him to re-discover the religious tradition and orthodoxy from which he thought he could escape.

Clive Staples Lewis was born in November 1898 in Belfast, Ireland to Albert and Flora Lewis. When Lewis was seven his family moved into a larger house, which they called "New House." As his health was delicate, he was not allowed outside for long periods of time and thus spent most of his childhood in the house.[42] In fact, said Lewis, "The New House is almost a major character in my story. I am a product of long corridors, empty sunlit rooms, upstairs indoor silences, attics explored in solitude, distant noises of gurgling cisterns and pipes, and the noise of wind under the tiles. Also, of endless books."[43] Spending so much time in the "New House" provided Lewis with two important things. First, it helped foster in him an appreciation for place and the imaginative largeness of his limited world.[44] Second, it provided him later with the setting for one of his best-loved books, *The*

39. Ibid., 6.
40. Lewis, *Surprised*, 58.
41. Ibid., 229.
42. Sayer, *Jack*, 35–36.
43. Lewis, *Surprised*, 10.
44. Though he came from a middle-class background, his frugality and—for a time—his tendency to give away a large portion of his income shows that Lewis's imaginative vision was not monetarily unfettered. Throughout his life, he fostered his imagination through books and nature walks, while still working full-time and living frugally. See Sayer, *Jack*, chapter 9, "Into Poverty."

Lion, the Witch, and the Wardrobe, which he expanded into a series of seven books that deal to a large degree with the issues of place and ethics, as I discuss in chapter 3.

Just as Chesterton's fascination with limits as a child acted as a key to fit the lock of his rediscovered orthodoxy, Lewis was also given a key, though of a different sort. Lewis's key was the experience of "joy." As a child, Lewis had three foundational episodes in which he experienced "joy" for the first time. The first occurred when his brother Warren showed him his toy garden consisting of a "biscuit tin filled with moss."[45] This took place when they still lived at the Old House. The toy garden awakened "desire," but for what he did not know, and the sensation was over in a "moment of time."[46] A second episode that reawakened the sensation of "joy" for Lewis came from reading *Squirrel Nutkin* by Beatrix Potter. Of this book and its corresponding emotions, Lewis states: "And one went back to the book, not to gratify the desire (that was impossible—how can one *possess* Autumn?) but to reawaken it. And in this experience also there was the same surprise and the same sense of incalculable importance. It was something quite different from everyday life and even from ordinary pleasure; something, as they would now say, 'in another dimension.'"[47]

The third encounter with "joy" occurred for Lewis from reading these lines in an "unrhymed translation of *Tegner's Drapa*: "I heard a voice that cried, | Balder the beautiful | Is dead, is dead—."[48] This third episode awakened a lifelong love for Northernness in Lewis. Of these three episodes, Lewis states, "[I]n a sense the central story of my life is about nothing else."[49] Lewis named this feeling he experienced "joy" and defined it as "that of an unsatisfied desire which is itself more desirable than any other satisfaction . . . and must be sharply distinguished both from Happiness and from Pleasure."[50] Throughout his childhood, adolescence, and early adulthood, Lewis pursued "joy" religiously, but found, much like John in his semi-autobiographical *Pilgrim's Regress*, that the experiences of "joy" became less frequent and intense. Once converted to Christianity, "the subject [had]

---

45. Lewis, *Surprised*, 16.
46. Ibid.
47. Ibid., 17.
48. Ibid.
49. Ibid.
50. Ibid., 17–18.

lost nearly all interest to [him]" (238). He viewed "joy" simply "as a pointer to something other and outer."[51]

What seems significant about the first glimpse of "joy" that Lewis felt as a child and what also links it to Chesterton's own childhood key is that it occurred through the medium of a toy, in this case a toy garden. The garden represented a small place, with very definite limits, but upon close imaginative inspection could open itself up as a whole world in and of itself. Unlike Chesterton, who found pleasure in his actual toy theater, Lewis seemed only interested in the feeling of "joy" brought on by the garden, thinking of the joy as another-worldly. For Lewis, the toy garden was a vehicle for the experience of desire, instead of a finite and physical object possessing its own value and beauty. He would learn to distinguish the difference later in his life.

Unlike Chesterton, whose childhood remained pleasant until he left home to go to school, Lewis's childhood gave way to sorrow much sooner. Perhaps the last key event that took place in Lewis's childhood that planted the seeds for his quest away from religious tradition and orthodoxy was the death of his mother in 1908 from abdominal cancer.[52] This traumatic event occurred when Lewis was eight and, as he described later, "was the occasion of what some (but not I) might regard as my first religious experience."[53] This is because, though he prayed fervently for his mother's healing during her decline towards death, and even after she died, hoping for a miracle, he "had approached God, or [his] idea of God, without love, without awe, even without fear."[54] In essence, he treated God as a "magician" and the disappointment left no lasting impression upon him.[55] With his mother's death the "old security" of home was lost and "[i]t was sea and islands now; the great continent had sunk like Atlantis."[56]

After his mother's death his father sent him away to school, where the seeds of his journey of discovery, away from religious tradition and orthodoxy, were nourished. He was sent to Wynyard School, where he was "taught" by a probably insane headmaster and was mentally and emotionally abused, as he extensively outlines in *Surprised by Joy*. However, it was

51. Ibid., 238.
52. Sayer, *Jack*, 47.
53. Lewis, *Surprised*, 20.
54. Ibid., 21.
55. Ibid.
56. Ibid.

here that he "first . . . became an effective believer."[57] To Saint John's, an Anglo-Catholic church, he was taken twice each Sunday. Though as an "Ulster Protestant" he chafed at the outward Catholic leanings of the church, it was there "that [he] heard the doctrines of Christianity (as distinct from general 'uplift') taught by men who obviously believed them."[58] Lewis's exposure to the "doctrines" and people who believed them suggest that the "influence of the church upon his intellect . . . became far more important than its influence on his feelings."[59] This period of religious fervor did not last long, however, as Wynyard was closed and Lewis was sent to Cherbourg School, where he was influenced by an occultist named Miss Cowie, the Matron. It is at this point that he "ceased to be a Christian."[60]

This rejection of Christian tradition and orthodoxy came about for two reasons. First, he prayed fervently, as before, but this time when his prayers were not answered, he began to doubt his faith and look elsewhere. His relationship with Cowie helped develop in him a "passion for the Occult," which he described as "a spiritual lust; and like the lust of the body it has the fatal power of making everything else in the world seem uninteresting while it lasts."[61] Here we see a similar principle at work as when he pursued "joy." Both goals were to experience something other-worldly, to take him out of his hum-drum experience and into something greater. This emphasis on feelings and discovering new things led him to "[alter] 'I believe' to 'one does feel.'"[62] Lewis during this period experienced the lingering Gnosticism in modernity that separates body and spirit. He had not yet gained a non-dualistic appreciation for the world that would form the foundation for a sacramental view, a view shared by Chesterton and Berry. This dualism is the second reason he lost faith in Christian doctrine and eventually began to call himself an "atheist."

There are many factors that contributed to Lewis's return to faith. Two of the most influential authors that helped were George MacDonald and Chesterton. Interestingly, MacDonald was a significant influence on Chesterton, so in essence he really influenced them both. For Lewis, this influence sprang from reading *Phantastes, a faerie Romance*. Lewis's later

57. Ibid., 33.
58. Ibid.
59. Sayer, *Jack*, 54.
60. Lewis, *Surprised*, 58.
61. Ibid., 60.
62. Ibid.

reflection on his experience with the book deserves to be quoted at length because it shows a significant development in his imagination regarding place:

> The woodland journeyings in that story, the ghostly enemies, the ladies both good and evil, were close enough to my habitual imagery to lure me on without the perception of a change . . . For in one sense the new country was exactly like the old . . . But in another sense all was changed . . . That night my imagination was, in a certain sense, baptized; the rest of me, not unnaturally, took longer. I had not the faintest notion what I had let myself in for by buying *Phantastes*.[63]

The type of imagination awakened in Lewis through his reading of MacDonald is a sacramental imagination. As stated earlier, a sacramental imagination is one that views the world as "good" and pointing to God as Creator. In other words, a sacramental imagination is implicitly teleological. A tree, for example, is not just millions of tightly packed atoms, but a visible signpost to a Creator who in goodness holds those atoms in place. A sacramental imagination places things within a larger cosmic order ordained by God. This imagination allowed Lewis, like Chesterton, to see and appreciate the world around him. Like the fairy tales that endow the commonplace with magical qualities, Lewis was able to see the good in his surroundings. He was able to see the inherent worth of things. Of course, I do not mean to imply that other traditions and faiths cannot see the worth in things or that their views are instrumentalizing. I am simply trying to show how a sacramental imagination allowed my authors to reject such views.

Chesterton's influence on Lewis's reasoning, however, was even greater than his influence on Lewis's imagination. Pre-Christian Lewis believed that "Chesterton had more sense than all the other moderns put together, bating, of course, his Christianity."[64] Chesterton, among others, helped Lewis to doubt his age's insistence on rejecting the past as outmoded, barbaric, and wrong compared to modern philosophies. Lewis's love for the classics helped add to this belief of his age, but he could not see how to bridge the past with the present. Here Chesterton helped Lewis bridge the gap: "Then I read Chesterton's *Everlasting Man* and for the first time saw the whole Christian outline of history set out in a form that seemed to me

---

63. Ibid., 179–81.
64. Ibid., 213.

to make sense."⁶⁵ Chesterton helped Lewis see how Christianity did not completely reject paganism, as the popular modern Christianity did, but instead fulfilled and built upon it as a foundation. For Lewis, "The question was no longer to find the one simply true religion among a thousand religions simply false. It was rather, 'Where has religion reached its true maturity? Where, if anywhere, have the hints of all Paganism been fulfilled?'"⁶⁶ Lewis, of course, decided that Christianity accomplished this and famously became, through some hyperbole of his own, "the most dejected and reluctant convert in all England," completing his journey home.⁶⁷ One could surmise that the dejection and reluctance came from swallowing his pride in accepting an orthodoxy he had resisted for so long. Lewis was persuaded because he recognized in orthodoxy not an outright rejection of history, but rather a fulfillment of it. In this sense orthodoxy is not a tiny box keeping safe its dogma from the world, but more like water, which permeates the world around it, providing life and health.

After accepting Christianity and its coherent worldview, Lewis was able to appreciate the present world around him, including "place." We can see this appreciation for place demonstrated in his cautions against rapid mobility. Like Chesterton, Lewis had a disdain for modern transportation for what it did to our ability to appreciate place. He states: "The truest and most horrible claim made for modern transport is that it "annihilates space." It does. It annihilates one of the most glorious gifts we have been given. It is a vile inflation which lowers the value of distance, so that a modern boy travels a hundred miles with less sense of liberation and pilgrimage and adventure than his grandfather got from traveling ten."⁶⁸ Lewis, like Chesterton, sees the rush of the modern age as an inhibitor to the ability to appreciate the world around us. Interestingly, he never learned to drive a car, though he tried to learn a couple of times and his groundskeeper often drove him back and forth between Oxford and his home.⁶⁹ Primarily, though, Lewis's feet were his main form of transportation, and he enjoyed both daily walks and occasional walking tours that afforded him the chance to enjoy the natural world. These daily walks offered Lewis the opportunity to exercise his sacramental imagination and see things not as instrumental,

---

65. Ibid., 223.
66. Ibid., 235.
67. Ibid., 228–29.
68. Ibid., 157.
69. Sayer, *Jack*, 202.

but as good. We will discuss in chapter 3 the implications of this new way of seeing things.

Like Chesterton and Lewis, Berry also faced a moment of crisis as a young man. Though many of his contemporary authors and artists in the United States during the mid-twentieth century were leaving their rural roots and congregating in major metropolitan areas to further their careers, he chose to reject this narrative in favor of returning to his native place. He was rejecting a cultural narrative that privileged mobility over rootedness and the city over the country. Over the course of the years following his return, Berry realized "how false and destructive and silly those ideas are."[70] In order to understand how Berry came to this countercultural point of view, one needs to look at his childhood and adolescence to see his development of a philosophy that privileges place.

Wendell Berry was born in Henry County, Kentucky, in 1934. The son of a lawyer, he grew up in the rural community of Port Royal, along the Kentucky River. Regarding religion, Berry states, "I was raised as a Southern Baptist. But I've always felt myself an outsider to the sects and denominations."[71] As anyone familiar with Berry would know, the town of Port William in which almost all of his fiction is set is based on the model of Port Royal, though of course it is not strictly autobiographical. Needless to say, Berry is a self-professed "placed" writer and, except for a few years of his early adulthood, he has resided within the same few miles of Kentucky. Those few years away from Henry County constitute a crucial moment in Berry's life narrative, as he could have easily chosen to remain away and become an "exiled" writer. Instead, he says, "I myself have traveled several thousand miles to arrive at Lane's Landing, five miles from where I was born, and the knowledge I gained by my travels was mainly that I was born into the same world as everybody else."[72] This rediscovery is similar to the phenomenon described earlier by Chesterton in *Orthodoxy*, of a man shipwrecked on a seemingly strange island only to discover that island is his English home.

Berry, like Chesterton and Lewis, also had a "key" passed on to him as a child. For Berry, this key was a cabin built along the Kentucky River by his great-uncle Curran Mathews. The cabin became known as the Camp. The significance of this dwelling was so great that Berry devoted a fifty-page

70. Berry, *Long-Legged*, 175.
71. *Christian Century*, "Toward," 912–16.
72. Berry, *Long-Legged*, 169.

autobiographical essay to it early in his literary career. Though his knowledge of Mathews from personal interaction was limited, as Mathews died when Berry was twelve or thirteen, Berry imaginatively pieced together a narrative of Mathews' life through his interaction with the cabin and landscaping he left behind. In fact, Mathews helped nurture young Berry's imagination by telling him "adventure stories," often borrowed from *Tarzan* or Zane Grey.[73] An adult Berry, though, imagines Mathews' thoughts as he built his two-room cabin by the river, interestingly acknowledging the imaginative impact of limits. He states:

> As soon as he [Mathews] marked out the dimensions of his house on the ground the place would have begun to look different to him, would have begun to have an intimacy for him that it could never have had before. Earlier, any place he stood was more or less equal to any other place he stood; he would move on to another place. But once those boundaries were marked on the ground, there would have begun to be a permanent allegiance.[74]

This "permanent allegiance" to the place has a direct metaphorical parallel in marriage and, like Chesterton, Berry seems to view both allegiances as a sort of romance. This romance is not unlike that felt by a young Chesterton with his toy theater or a young Lewis with his toy garden—the boundaries enhanced, to twist a phrase, "captive imaginations."

Like Chesterton and Lewis, Berry had discovered a "world" of fixed limits, and this similarly shaped his imagination. Though Mathews' decision to build the Camp along the river was partially due to health reasons, Berry insisted that "the best reason for the cabin he built . . . must be that it was in his nature to have a house built in the woods and to return now again to live in it. For there was something deep about him, something quiet-loving and solitary and kin to the river and the woods."[75] One would think Berry was describing himself. How did Berry's relationship with the Camp begin? Interestingly, as a boy he found the cabin an escape from adult supervision, a retreat in which he could make his own rules, much as his bachelor great-uncle did. To Berry "[i]t was the family's wilderness place, and lay beyond the claims and disciplines and obligations that motivated my grownups."[76] It was here that he escaped, often alone, sometimes with

73. Ibid., 119, 109.
74. Ibid., 113.
75. Ibid., 110.
76. Ibid., 115.

his brother or friends, and canoed, read *Walden*, and camped. When he was "nearly fourteen" he slept there alone one night and it was then, he says, that there "began a conscious relation between me and the Camp, and it has been in my mind and figured in my plans ever since."[77] So much so that he fixed up the Camp in the days leading up to his wedding and he and his new bride Tanya made it their first home together the summer they were married. Of this he says, "Our marriage became then, and has remained, the center of our life. And it is particularly true that the Camp is the center of our marriage, both as actuality and as symbol."[78]

However, the seeds had already been planted in his mind to move away from the Camp. An earlier memory of when he was fishing in the river highlights this change. As he was fishing, enjoying the moment, he suddenly became aware of what he was doing, causing him to be "deeply uneasy, even distressed."[79] He attributes this unease to the messages taught to him by culture: "My cultural inheritance had prepared me to exert myself, work, move, 'get someplace.' To be idle, simply to live there in the sunlight in the middle of the river, was something I was not prepared to do deliberately."[80] This cultural demand of oughts caused the "spell" to be "broken."[81] A major cultural narrative that influenced Berry was the narrative that all rural children should go to college, get educated, move permanently to the city to get jobs, and thus "advance" their positions. So, in the fall of 1957 Berry and Tanya moved to Georgetown, Kentucky where he taught at Georgetown College for two years. Then, from 1959 to 1960, Berry taught creative writing at Stanford University in California. He then spent a year traveling Europe on a Guggenheim Fellowship, before teaching at New York University from 1962 to 1964.[82]

While in New York, Berry decided to return to Kentucky and accepted a teaching position at the University of Kentucky. Understandably, this decision was not an easy one and numerous family, friends, and colleagues tried to convince him to stay in New York. He says, "The decision to leave had cost me considerable difficulty and doubt and hard thought—for hadn't I achieved what had become one of the most traditional goals of American

77. Ibid., 119–20.
78. Ibid., 130.
79. Ibid., 123.
80. Ibid.
81. Ibid.
82. Grubbs, *Conversations*, xviii.

writers? I had reached the greatest city in the nation; I had a good job; I was meeting with other writers and talking to them and learning from them; I had reason to hope that I might take a still larger part in the literary life of that place."[83] However, Berry, who was still writing about Kentucky, could not "escape" it: "Kentucky was my fate."[84] He says, "I still had a deep love for the place I had been born in, and liked the idea of going back to be a part of it again."[85] A senior faculty member in his department, "speak[ing] . . . as a representative of the literary world," tried to convince him to stay.[86] Of this faculty member's mindset, Berry states:

> I do not pretend to know all about the other man's mind . . . His argument was based on the belief that once one had attained the metropolis, the literary capital, the worth of one's origins was cancelled out; there simply could be nothing *worth* going back to. What lay behind me . . . had become "subject matter." And there was the belief, long honored among American intellectuals and artists and writers, that a place such as I came from could only be returned to at the price of intellectual death . . . Finally, there was the assumption that the life of the metropolis is *the* experience, the *modern* experience . . ."[87]

Central to this urban assumption is an implied rootlessness ("cancelled out") that suggests a person's development—intellectual, creative, or otherwise—exists in a vacuum, as if a person could make him or herself from nothing. Also implied here is a clear utilitarianism about "one's origins," as they are only extrinsically meaningful as steps along the way to the "*modern* experience."

In contrast, says Berry, "the life of the rural towns, the farms, the wilderness places is not only irrelevant to our time, but archaic as well because unknown or unconsidered by the people who really matter—that is, urban intellectuals."[88] Berry labels these ideas "false and destructive and silly."[89] He acknowledges his awareness that there was literary precedent for what he decided to do: "if there was Wolfe, there was also Faulkner; if there was

---

83. Berry, *Long-Legged*, 174.
84. Ibid.
85. Ibid.
86. Ibid., 175.
87. Ibid.
88. Ibid.
89. Ibid.

James, there was also Thoreau."⁹⁰ What made the "greatest difference" in his decision "was the knowledge of the few square miles in Kentucky that were mine by inheritance and by birth and by the intimacy the mind makes with the place it awakens in."⁹¹ So he returned to Kentucky and, once "settled," he "began to see the place with a new clarity and a new understanding and a new seriousness."⁹² He "began to see the real abundance and richness of it."⁹³ Eventually, he reached the point where he viewed himself "as growing out of the earth like the other native animals and plants,"⁹⁴ just as Chesterton did when he noted earlier that when "we are rooted in place ... [w]e live like a tree with the whole strength of the universe."⁹⁵

After he returned to his home along the Kentucky River, Berry began to ask questions: "What *is* this place? What is in it? What is its nature? How should men live in it? What must I do?"⁹⁶ He viewed these questions as "a part of the necessary enactment of humility, teaching a man what his importance is, what his responsibility is, and what his place is, both on the earth and in the order of things."⁹⁷ He calls these questions "moral," "aesthetic," "practical," and "religious," though he is "uneasy" using the term "religious."⁹⁸ Unlike many Enlightenment and post-Enlightenment thinkers who do not reflect upon the Judeo-Christian tradition foundational to their beliefs, Berry in his reflecting has reached this foundational "religious" level.⁹⁹ Here he wrestles with his own culturally Baptist religious heritage,

90. Ibid., 175–76.
91. Ibid., 176.
92. Ibid., 177.
93. Ibid.
94. Ibid., 178.
95. Chesterton, *Heretics*, 22.
96. Berry, *Long-Legged*, 199.
97. Ibid.

98. Ibid. As discussed in the introduction, many scholars see Berry as orthodox and Christian, acknowledging that even though he might not explicitly declare his faith like Chesterton and Lewis do in their apologetics, that does not mean his writings do not implicitly exhibit these religious beliefs. For example, Cloutier, "Working," 614, states, "What do we need to see in the American context, specifically, especially to make the connections among the grammar of these often-separated areas of Catholic ethics? In the American context, I contend that there is no better interpreter than the farmer, poet, and essayist Wendell Berry." Likewise, Peters, "Education," 274–75, labels Berry's anti-Gnosticism "*orthodox*." See also the recent edited collection of essays *Wendell Berry and Religion: Heaven's Earthly Life*.

99. For example, Taylor, *Sources of the Self*, 96, claims, "The story of the Exodus

that "has promoted and fed upon the destructive schism between body and soul, heaven and earth" and "encouraged people to believe that the world is of no importance, and that their only obligation in it is to submit to certain churchly formulas in order to get to heaven."[100] For Berry, this type of religion has led to the thoughtless destruction of nature, because it removes "the creator" from "the creation."[101] "For these reasons," says Berry, "though I know that my questions *are* religious, I dislike having to *say* that they are."[102] He next explains how his questions spring from a different religious philosophy:

> But when I ask them my aim is not primarily to get to heaven. Though heaven is certainly more important than the earth if all they say about it is true, it is still morally incidental to it and dependent on it, and I can only imagine it and desire it in terms of what I know of the earth. And so my questions do not aspire beyond the earth. They aspire toward it and into it. Perhaps they aspire through it. They are religious because they are asked at the limit of what I know; they acknowledge mystery and honor its presence in the creation; they are spoken in reverence for the order and grace that I see, and that I trust beyond my power to see.[103]

This insight, in some ways, seems similar to what Lewis learned from reading *Phantastes*: to not look for joy by despising the earth through looking always beyond it, but instead to see how it is expressed all around us on earth. This statement is the expression of a sacramental imagination, which values things for themselves and not as instruments to help us get along to our "real home."

Finally, like Chesterton and Lewis in their caution about the modern fascination with automobiles, Berry is also resistant to fast technology that

---

has inspired movements of reform and liberation throughout the centuries, even those which claim to reject the theological outlook which the original story proclaims ... Even where the theology is lost, the story marches on. Northrop Frye shows how the Bible as a whole has been a tremendous source of such empowering stories in Western history." The writings of Chesterton, Lewis, and Berry can be seen as asking, "What if the theological component of this tradition is essential to helping moderns understand and navigate their world?"

100. Berry, *Long-Legged*, 199.//
101. Ibid.//
102. Ibid., 200.//
103. Ibid.

reduces "place" to "scenery."[104] In the early essay "The Nature Consumers," Berry laments the weekender/vacationer pleasure boating that takes place on and along the Kentucky River, of which he has a front-row view from his house. In this case, then, the technology that Berry sees as harmful to our perception of place is speedboats. He admits that racing a powerful engine can have a thrill in and of its own and he has no problem with this, though he thinks if this thrill is all boaters are after they should limit themselves to a small stretch of river in which to race and leave the rest of the river at peace.[105] The problem, though, is that these boaters do not limit themselves and they become "consumers of the river."[106] Berry likens their "destructiveness" to that "of certain industries, and it has the same causes: the use of powerful machines, and the discarding of more or less imperishable refuse."[107] This makes the boatman "what more and more seems the ideal man of our society: a superconsumer" because his "pursuit of pleasure is determined and limited not by his and his family's need but by the size and speed of his boat, and so he takes far more than he needs."[108] For Berry, the boatman "has become a symbol . . . of an alienation from the world that I believe to be common among us, and on the increase. Because he could not be still, the place could not exist for him."[109] This is because, "[l]ike all country places, [Berry's valley] is both complex and reticent. It cannot be understood by passing through,"[110] just as Chesterton stated earlier that China and Arabia "are ancient civilizations with strange virtues buried like treasures" and should not be abstracted to scenery.[111] The boatman has turned the places around him into "scenery," defined by Berry as "an oversimplification and falsification of nature."[112] This perspective divorces humans from nature, turning nature into an "other," which of course often leads to abuses. This modern mentality is a false dichotomy, says Berry:

> Man cannot be independent of nature. In one way or another he must live in relation to it, and there are only two alternatives: the

104. Ibid., 40.
105. Ibid., 38.
106. Ibid., 35.
107. Ibid.
108. Ibid., 38.
109. Ibid., 32.
110. Ibid., 33.
111. Chesterton, *Heretics*, 23.
112. Berry, *Long-Legged*, 40.

> way of the frontiersman, whose response to nature was to dominate it, to assert his presence in it by destroying it; or the way of Thoreau, who went to the natural places to become quiet in them, to learn from them, to be restored by them. To know these places, because to know them is to need them and respect them and be humble before them, is to preserve them. To fail to know them, because ignorance can only be greedy of them, is to destroy them.[113]

Unlike the popular strain in Christianity that sees in Genesis a command to subdue and take dominion of the earth, Berry is here offering a significant corrective that emphasizes the non-dualistic, interdependent relationship between humans and nature.

Thus far, we have examined how Chesterton, Lewis, and Berry wrestled with questions of identity in their young adult lives. These questions led them first away from their spiritual roots but then eventually back to them, not through resigned acceptance, but after careful intellectual consideration. For Berry, this return was physical as well. This theme of homecoming is evident not only in the personal biographies and non-fiction writings of the three authors, but also in their fiction. Three good examples are Chesterton's *Manalive*, Lewis's *Pilgrim's Regress*, and Berry's *Jayber Crow*. Examining the theme of homecoming in these three novels will help us understand the sought-for integration of their lives and values within particular times, situations, and places. Understanding the particularities of this integration is a valuable component of the humanities.

Homecoming and Return
in *Manalive*, *Pilgrim's Regress*, and *Jayber Crow*

Chesterton's 1912 novel *Manalive* is a key text in his canon because it presents us with two competing philosophies of life—that of its protagonist Innocent Smith and the despair of the *fin de siècle*. In fact, it is Smith's rejection of this opposing philosophy that leads him to appreciate places and limits.

The novel is divided into two parts. In part one, Smith chases his hat on an extremely windy day into the yard of Beacon House, where he surprises its seven inhabitants by his spontaneous exuberance for life and eccentric behavior. He requests a room for the night. While he is there, one of the other lodgers, Mary Gray, becomes smitten with Smith and agrees to

113. Ibid., 42.

leave with him by hansom cab to go visit his aunt. Before they can leave, however, another lodger returns with an American detective and four criminal charges against Smith. In part two, a trial is held in Beacon House, whereby the four charges against Smith are explained, but dismissed when new evidence is introduced by the defense. Cleared, Smith and Gray leave with another strong gust of wind.

For Chesterton, Smith represents a celebration of life and the limits that go along with it. Smith is a direct affront to the modern pessimism of the age that, having rejected the orthodoxies and traditions of the past and having no clear vision of the future, finally despairs of life itself. As his name implies, Innocent is wide-eyed and childlike in his appreciation of the world around him. "Smith" implies he represents everyman and his initials on his suitcase, "I. S.," emphasize Chesterton's main philosophical point: the wonder of birth, of existence. This personality trait alone would cause one to think of Chesterton; Smith's description does so as well, as he is described as "a large light-haired man in gay green holiday clothes" who had a "shape generally gigantesque."[114] Iain T. Benson says of this similarity, "They are both larger than life, outside any academic rule, and sweep exuberantly onto the scene with a mission to wake up an altogether sleeping world around themselves."[115]

Depicting a malaise similar to that found in Woolf's as yet unwritten *Voyage Out*, Chesterton's sleeping world consists of seven characters aimlessly residing in the boarding house. Having rejected an orthodoxy that might have provided them with a *telos*, they instead mindlessly busy themselves with the details of "ordinary life," from the mundane to the shocking.[116] In the novel, Smith's character is described as bringing these seven separate people together: "An hour ago, and for four years previously, these people had avoided each other, even when they really liked each other. They had slid in and out of dismal and deserted rooms in search of particular

---

114. Chesterton, *Manalive*, 270.

115. Benson, Introduction, 26.

116. Taylor, *Sources of the Self*, 211, states, "'Ordinary life' is a term of art I introduce to designate those aspects of human life concerned with production and reproduction, that is, labour, the making of the things needed for life, and our life as sexual beings, including marriage and the family . . . For Aristotle the maintenance of these activities was to be distinguished from the pursuit of the good life. They are, of course, necessary to the good life, but they play an infrastructural role in relation to it. You can't pursue the good life without pursuing life. *But an existence dedicated to this latter goal alone is not a fully human one*" (emphasis mine).

newspapers and private needlework. Even now they all came casually, as with varying interests; but they all came."[117] One of the lodgers, Michael Moon, who is known for being "wild," demonstrates the impact Smith has on all of them when he says to another lodger, Arthur Inglewood, "If you have heard that I am wild, you can contradict the rumour . . . I am tame . . . I drink too much of the same kind of whisky at the same time every night. I even drink about the same amount too much."[118] After saying the same things about going to the "same public-houses," "meet[ing] the same damned women" and "hear[ing] the same . . . dirty stories," he states matter-of-factly, "You may reassure my friends, Inglewood, you see before you a person whom civilization has thoroughly tamed."[119] In reply, Inglewood claims Moon's behavior is normal in a world he "finds . . . a bit dull."[120] Here Moon interrupts, "That fellow doesn't . . . I mean that fellow Smith. I have a fancy there's some method in his madness. It looks as if he could turn into a sort of wonderland any minute by taking one step out of the plain road . . . Perhaps that is the real key of fairyland."[121]

Eventually, the motley crew discovers the "method in his madness": Chesterton is fictionalizing the astonishing homecoming from *Orthodoxy*. We see this throughout Smith's trial. After Smith quickly woos one of the lodgers, Mary Gray, the two of them plan to take a trip together. However, before they can do so, another lodger, Dr. Warner, returns to the house with a "criminal specialist" from America named Dr. Cyras Pym.[122] The two of them accuse Smith of (attempted) murder, burglary, deserting his family, and polygamy. Moon takes up Smith's defense and in each case is able to show how Smith is indeed innocent of the charges, though admittedly by living an unconventional life. The three charges that are most concerned with homecoming are the latter three: in each case he has left his home and returned, so therefore he is "burglarizing" his own house, returning (after a period) to his family, and "remarrying" his own wife by wooing her as if she were a stranger. In fact, Mary Gray turns out to be his wife, though under an assumed name. Why does Smith do these unconventional and seemingly crazy things? He does them so that he can appreciate his home

117. Chesterton, *Manalive*, 276.
118. Ibid., 283.
119. Ibid.
120. Ibid.
121. Ibid.
122. Ibid., 310.

and wife with that sense of wonder one feels with new things—he does not want to become accustomed to them, or bored with them, as Inglewood and Moon are bored with the world. In other words, Smith is living out the feeling of discovering a "new" place only to discover it is an old, familiar place, like Chesterton's fictional man who discovered England at the beginning of *Orthodoxy*. Chesterton wants to underscore through Smith's life the importance of loving and appreciating not only life, but one's home, or place on the earth.

Perhaps the clearest example of the connection between love of place and love of existence for Chesterton is found in one of the letters read for Smith's defense of the desertion charge. The letter writer, Louis, narrates a conversation he had with Smith while they stood on a rock formation overlooking a ravine under the stars. Louis tells Smith:

> "'My grandmother,' I said in a low tone, 'would have said that we were all in exile, and that no earthly house could cure the holy homesickness that forbids us rest.' . . .
>
> Then he said: 'I think your grandmother was right,' and stood up leaning on his grassy pole. 'I think that must be the reason,' he said—'the secret of this life of man, so ecstatic and so unappeased. But I think there is more to be said. I think God has given us the love of special places, of a hearth and of a native land, for a good reason.'
>
> "'I dare say,' I said. 'What reason?'
>
> "'Because otherwise,' he said, pointing his pole out at the sky and the abyss, 'we might worship that.'
>
> "'What do you mean?' I demanded.
>
> "'Eternity,' he said in his harsh voice, 'the largest of the idols—the mightiest of the rivals of God.'"[123]

Here Smith, a clear representative of Chesterton himself, emphasizes the necessity of places and "native land" in the lives of humans. It is significant that God's absolute transcendence is in tension with the Incarnation, giving value to things of earth, because this underscores the necessity of place in the teleology of humans. Also, the contrast between places and eternity is important. As mentioned earlier, Arendt made a similar claim in *The Human Condition*, that one of the "commonplace" desires of modern humans was expressed in a current newspaper report about a 1957 satellite launch: to "'escape from men's imprisonment to the earth.'"[124] This desire

---

123. Ibid., 398.

124. Arendt, *Human Condition*, 1.

to escape the human condition, she explains, can be seen in the distinction between "immortal" and "eternal." Classically, humans were concerned with being immortal: living forever through their deeds expressed generation after generation on earth.[125] In contrast, eternity is a state unique and separate from the human condition: it is a quality of God, whereas immortality was a quality of gods.[126] Arendt and Chesterton seem to be in agreement that by striving after eternity, humans desire to rival God by escaping their human condition. Last, we can see in this passage a summing up of a central component to Chesterton's homecoming, by bringing together two important points of emphasis. First, this passage emphasizes the desire for something eternal and therefore unattainable on earth. Second, this passage also emphasizes, and draws our attention to, the good of the world. Bringing these two emphases together counterbalances the excessive pride pervading the pursuit of the infinite.

In 1933, Lewis published *The Pilgrim's Regress*, one of his earliest published works. As the title indicates, it is an allegory in the vein of Bunyan's *The Pilgrim's Progress*. The story centers on John, who was born into Puritania, a land run by Stewards for the Landlord. As a youth, John discovers a vision of an island that awakens in him desire. He decides to reject and disobey the Landlord and leave Puritania to search for the Island. He meets numerous characters on his journey, such as Mr. Enlightenment, Mr. Mammon, Mr. Sensible, Savage, and Mr. Broad, who all try to help him view the world as they do. Mr. Vertue joins John in his quest and they find that a Grand Canyon separates them from their destination. Mother Kirk offers to carry them across, but they refuse and suffer on their own for quite some time. Eventually, the hermit History helps instruct John about the Pagans, Shepherds, and the man Nomos who bridges the two, and John accepts the help of Mother Kirk. He finds that Mr. Vertue has done the same, and each is instructed to slay the North and South Dragons, respectively. After slaying his dragon, John is sent back home to Puritania to live until the Landlord calls him across the Grand Canyon again.

As seen earlier, Lewis credited George MacDonald's *Phantastes* with "baptizing" his imagination. Recently, Jeffrey Bilbro has shown extensive parallels between MacDonald's *Phantastes* and Lewis's *The Pilgrim's Regress*.[127] He states, "Where MacDonald lays out this path without attempt-

---

125. Ibid., 19.
126. Ibid., 18–20.
127. Bilbro, "Phantastical Regress," 22, summarizes the similarities as such: "The

ing to justify it, Lewis traces this path on the map of western philosophy, arguing for its validity and attempting to show how the themes present in MacDonald—romanticism, selfless action, and Christian redemption—can be synthesized with this philosophic tradition."[128] According to Andrew Wheat, "*The Pilgrim's Regress* is one of the best guides to Lewis' thought because, in spite of its apparent shortcomings, it is a masterful illustration (not simply codification) of a conversion. It shows that life is a quest, not merely a string of questions."[129]

However, Lewis allows for completing the journey in a much shorter way than John (and Lewis). As a child, John watched his Uncle George cross a brook and enter the Landlord's estate, while he, his parents, and their Steward saw him off. In contrast, John went the opposite direction of the Landlord's estate, in search of the Island. Thus he began a long and painful journey in which he had to confront and battle the numerous philosophies of the present and past. He finds, however, that he ironically ends up where he had hoped to escape:

> 'Thank you,' said John. 'Pray, do we take ship from here?'
>
> But Slikisteinsauga [John and Vertue's Guide] shook his head: and he asked them to look at the Island again and specifically to consider the shape . . . to which it rose at its highest point.
>
> 'I see,' said John presently.
>
> 'What do you see?' said the Guide.
>
> 'They are the very same shape as that summit of the Eastern Mountain which we called the Landlord's castle as we saw it from Puritania.'
>
> 'They are not only the same shape. They are the same.'
>
> 'How can that be?' said John with a sinking heart, 'for those mountains were in the extreme East, and we have been travelling West ever since we left home.'
>
> 'But the world is round . . . the Island is the other side of the Mountains, and not . . . an Island at all.'[130]

Here John asks how they are to go forward with their journey. He gets some disappointing news, as the Guide who "looked at him as a merciful

---

protagonists of both books travel similar paths: both are drawn on their journeys by an inexplicable longing, both are linked to a knight or armed man, and both must embrace death before accomplishing deeds of valor on their journey home."

128. Ibid., 22–23.

129. Wheat, "Road Before Him," 36.

130. Lewis, *Pilgrim's*, 131.

man looks on an animal which he must hurt" tells him, "The way to go on ... is to go back."[131] To this John resigns himself: "What must be must be ... I deserve no better. You mean that I have been wasting my labour all my life, and I have gone half-round the world to reach what Uncle George reached in a mile or so."[132] The Guide replies, "Who knows what your uncle has reached, except the Landlord? Who knows what you would have reached if you had crossed the brook without ever leaving home? You may be sure the Landlord has brought you the shortest way: though I confess it would look an odd journey on a map."[133]

Interestingly, what Lewis discovered in his own journey and what he communicates through John's is that in pursuing Joy or an Island to fulfill the longing inside of them, they thought they would escape their homes, earth, or in Arendt's terms "the human condition." Instead, once converted or baptized, Christianity sends them back into the very condition they thought they were escaping. Christianity sends them home, at least until death.[134] This is because the Kingdom of God is not "out of this world," but rather coexists with reality. It is the "present, not yet," forecasting Christ's return as the *telos* for the creation. So Christianity gives its adherents new eyes to see the world in its relationship to its creator (sacramentally, as we saw earlier in Berry). Therefore, both Lewis and John's view of the world is changed: as the Guide tells John, "I should warn you of one thing—the country will look very different on the return journey."[135] According to Slikisteinsauga, they see "the land as it really is."[136] This change is not com-

---

131. Ibid.
132. Ibid.
133. Ibid.
134. Ibid., 132. Relevant to his view of the afterlife, Lewis in *Letters to Malcolm*, 92–93, states: "I do not think that the life of Heaven bears any analogy to play or dance in respect to frivolity. I do think that while we are in this 'valley of tears,' cursed with labour, hemmed round with necessities, tripped up with frustrations, doomed to perpetual plannings, puzzlings, and anxieties, certain qualities that must belong to the celestial condition have no chance to get through, can project no image of themselves. For surely we must suppose the life of the blessed to be an end in itself, indeed The End: to be utterly spontaneous; to be the complete reconciliation of boundless freedom with order—with the most delicately adjusted, supple, intricate, and beautiful order . . . Joy is the serious business of Heaven." In light of this view of heaven, Lewis's mature view of the Christian life is that it does not cease to have labor, but that after conversion Christians can see glimpses of Heaven even in the frivolities of life.
135. Lewis, *Pilgrim's*, 132.
136. Ibid., 134.

pletely welcome, either. John states, "I think Mother Kirk treats us very ill. Since we have followed her and eaten her food the way seems twice as narrow and twice as dangerous as it did before."[137] The Guide replies, "You all know . . . that security is mortals' greatest enemy."[138]

After retracing their steps and slaying their respective dragons, the three find themselves before an "empty and ruinous" cottage in Puritania.[139] John cries, because it is his "father's house" and his parents have "gone already beyond the brook."[140] The Guide informs him that he will join his parents by nightfall, whereupon Vertue seeks to comfort him by reciting a poem that embraces Gods' sovereignty over death. John replies, "I thought all those things when I was in the house of Wisdom. But now I think better things. Be sure it is not for nothing that the Landlord has knit our hearts so closely to time and place—to one friend rather than another and one shire more than all the land."[141] Then he recites his own poem:

> 'Passing to-day by a cottage, I shed tears
> When I remembered how once I had dwelled there
> With my mortal friends who are dead. Years
> Little had healed the wound that was laid bare.
>
> 'Out, little spear that stabs. I, fool, believed
> I had outgrown the local, unique sting,
> I had transmuted away (I was deceived)
> Into love universal the lov'd thing.
>
> 'But Thou, Lord, surely knewest Thine own plan
> When the angelic indifferences with no bar
> Universally loved but Thou gav'st man
> The tether and pang of the particular;
>
> 'Which, like a chemic drop, infinitesimal,
> Plashed into pure water, changing the whole,
> Embodies and embitters and turns all
> Spirit's sweet water to astringent soul.

137. Ibid.
138. Ibid.
139. Ibid., 151.
140. Ibid.
141. Ibid., 152.

'That we, though small, may quiver with fire's same
Substantial form as Thou—nor reflect merely,
As lunar angel, back to thee, cold flame.
Gods we are, Thou has said: and we pay dearly.'[142]

In this poem, John expresses a significant difference between humans and angels. Part of being made in the image of God means that humans, unlike angels, can feel "[t]he tether and pang of the particular." Seeing the home of his youth, John is reminded that humans are given the "local" and "unique sting" of feeling sadness for the loss of "mortal friends" with whom one has "dwelled." This "unique" aspect is shared by God and humans and is manifest in humans when God (the Landlord) "knit[s] our hearts so closely to time and place—to one friend rather than another and one shire more than all the land."[143] This aspect of humanity brings with it both joy and sorrow, pleasure and pain, but is not something that John (or Lewis) seems to despise. Rather, Lewis seems to accept this aspect of humanity as a part of the human condition, much as Berry does when he tries to explain why he has chosen to live in the part of Kentucky where he grew up. For both, the being born into a place makes this connection—not chance, per se, because both believe that God does the "knitting." This emphasis on the particular stands in contrast with the universal rights and freedoms many push for today, which do not recognize the contradictions often inherent in particularities.

Wendell Berry's 2000 novel, *Jayber Crow*, continues the theme of returning to place that he discussed in *The Long Legged House*. The novel is the first-person account of Jayber Crow, the barber of Port William. Jayber is born in 1914 in the small town of Goforth, Kentucky, just outside of Port Royal. After the death of his parents he is placed under the care of first his aunt and then, when she dies, a religious orphanage called The Good Shepherd "in the central part of the state."[144] This religious environment helps him feel the "call" to be a pastor; so when Jayber is old enough he goes to Pigeonville College to study to become one. However, while there he discovers he does not really have the "call;" so he drops out and moves to the city of Lexington where he finds work as a barber and takes a couple of classes at the university there. Jayber decides to give up the academic life

---

142. Ibid.
143. Ibid.
144. Berry, *Jayber*, 30.

and he returns home to Port Royal, where he finds it is in need of a barber. All of this takes place in the first hundred pages of the novel. The remaining three hundred pages deal with his life as the barber of the community of Port William, specifically with his relationship with Mattie Keith. Due to its meager salary, Jayber's role as the community barber condemns him to bachelorhood in the eyes of the community. Therefore, though he falls in love with Mattie, he must watch helplessly as she marries Troy Chatham, who rejects her father's traditional farm ways to become a modern agribusiness farmer, though it financially ruins them. Jayber never reveals his feelings to Mattie and his "marriage" to her is platonic, only existing in his thoughts. However, the story ends with Mattie's slow death in a hospital while Jayber, not Troy, is by her side because Troy is cutting down her favorite forest to pay off financial debts.

In this novel, the concept of homecoming manifests itself in two primary ways: first, literally in that Jayber returns to the community he was born into, Port William, and second, metaphorically in that Jayber decides to return to and commit to Mattie in his secret "marriage." This metaphorical reading is no surprise, as Berry has long stressed the similarities of marriage between people and choosing one place over another (or all others). For example, one of his best short stories, discussed below in chapter 4, is titled "Fidelity." Also, as mentioned earlier, Berry said marriage "has remained, the center of our life."[145]

Once Jayber had decided to live in Port William and be its barber, his journey homeward was still not complete. He physically resided in one specific place by making a home in Port William, but mentally he had not yet devoted himself to that place. As he was a young bachelor, he had the desire for the company of women[146] and to go carousing in night spots. As he puts it, "Back in those days I still wanted to take an active part in the ongoing life of the twentieth century, and so two or three years after the war [WWII] I bought a car."[147] Why did he need a car, a symbol of twentieth century technological modernity that, as we have seen, was a concern for Chesterton, Lewis, and Berry? Cars were symptomatic of a larger modern social issue: "The old homemade Saturday nights, when they would carry the furniture out into the yard and roll up the rugs and dance until sunup, were gone and done for. Now especially the young ones wanted to jump

---

145. Berry, *Long-Legged*, 130.
146. Berry, *Jayber*, 171.
147. Ibid., 166.

into a car on Saturday night and run down to Hargrave where whiskey and beer were legal and there were picture shows and places where you could drink and listen to the jukebox and dance."[148] In other words, rural people in twentieth century America were no longer entertaining themselves in their local communities, but were driving to cities to socialize for a price: "There was always something of interest going on that you had to pay to get into."[149] So Jayber bought himself a Dodge Zephyr.

Purchasing this new technology and incorporating it into his life bring about several changes. First, he does not really need it. When the car's previous owner asks, "Boy, where have *you* got any business going?," he has no answer.[150] Previously, Jayber had travelled almost exclusively by walking and this is still sufficient to meet his needs, as everything from food, to shelter, to business, to socializing is available to him within Port William. In fact, even Hargrave is within walking distance. Second, having a car takes resources such as energy, attention, and money from Jayber just by being in his possession. He states, "After I had bought it, I was secretly a little horrified by it. When I was not driving it, which was nearly all the time, it sat with a complacent expression in the driveway beside the shop, seeming to be eating and digesting my money."[151] Financially, Jayber has to pay for fuel, maintenance, repairs, and to keep it clean. Mentally and emotionally, he worries over his car, babying it by not driving it very far or very fast. The car is a liability. Eventually, Jayber decides to forsake this technology and tether himself to the community of Port William.

Significantly, this decision to give up his car coincides with his decision to commit to Mattie and be faithful. Through Jayber's escapades in Hargrave, he meets and begins dating a woman named Clydie. Jayber likes Clydie, perhaps even loves her, but he has already fallen in love with Mattie before he met Clydie. While at a Christmas dance in Hargrave with Clydie, Jayber sees Troy dancing with a woman who is obviously not Mattie. Troy sees Jayber and gives him "a wink and a grin, raising his hand to [Jayber] with the thumb and forefinger joined in a circle."[152] This causes Jayber to stop dancing with Clydie and feel sick to his stomach. He is sickened because of the knowledge that Troy was unfaithful to Mattie, but that is not all.

148. Ibid.
149. Ibid., 167.
150. Ibid.
151. Ibid.
152. Ibid., 237.

He is also sickened by the realization that he and Troy may be more similar than he wants to admit: "But I was thinking too, as Troy winked at me and raised his sign: 'We're *not* alike!' And that was what sickened me, because I wasn't sure."[153] Admittedly, Jayber is drunk, so that may explain his next actions, but I think the depth of his inner thought shows enough clarity for us to take his decisions seriously. Jayber excuses himself from Clydie and goes to the men's room, where he decides to climb out of the window and walk back to Port William rather than face her in his intoxicated, sickened state. Perhaps we are to read in his actions that Jayber feels guilt for being as unfaithful as Troy, both to Mattie and to Clydie. Before he walks home, he leaves a farewell message in the front seat of his car for Clydie, leaving the keys to the car for her. The Zephyr becomes a parting gift.

On his walk home that night, Jayber makes two commitments that forever alter the course of his life. He decides that he does not want to end up like Troy and that Mattie deserves to have a faithful husband. He therefore decides to commit to her, to become that faithful husband that she needs, even if she never knows. The decision works itself out in a moving internal dialogue that ends in a wedding vow:

> "You love her enough to be a faithful husband to her? Think what you're saying, now. You're proposing to be the faithful husband of a woman who is already married to an unfaithful husband?"
>
> "Yes. That's why. If she has an unfaithful husband, then she needs a faithful one."
>
> "A woman already married who must never know that you are her husband? Think. And who will never be your wife?"
>
> "Yes."
>
> "Have you foreseen how this may end? Can you?"
>
> "No."
>
> "Are you ready for this? Think now."
>
> "Yes. I am ready."
>
> "Do you, then, in love's mystery and fear, give yourself to this woman to be her faithful husband from this day forward, for better for worse, for richer for poorer, in sickness and in health, till death?"
>
> "I do. Yes! That is my vow."[154]

In committing to Mattie, Jayber also commits to Port William, because he has relinquished both his car (symbolic of the freedom and means

---

153. Ibid., 238.
154. Ibid., 243.

to engage with the modern world) and his girlfriend (and any future chance of having a family). Jayber's vow becomes his double homecoming, manifested in his commitments to a person and a place. Jayber keeps his vow and the novel ends with Jayber, not Troy, by Mattie's side when she breathes her last in a hospital bed.

After briefly looking at narratives of homecoming in the personal biographies and fiction of Chesterton, Lewis, and Berry, a few important similarities emerge in their deep attachment to and affection for place. First, all three authors emphasize that the process of accepting one's place involves an often difficult but necessary choice. Second, this choice involves accepting the limits that necessarily accompany place and therefore certain modern things, such as automobiles, may need to be rejected or more thoughtfully used. Third, one's perception of the world changes when one chooses to stay rooted in a place, be it religious, physical, or both.

For the common-place person, leaving one's home to return may be necessary to see it in this new way. A mobile lifestyle of discovery rejects and depreciates the past/home and this leads to problems, like those found in the Christian trope of longing for heaven (as the real home) at the expense and detriment of the earth (a necessary evil). As we will see more fully in a moment, we cannot label our environment as other, if we choose to stay rooted in our commitment to it. However, choosing to return home is only the first step, because doing so necessitates certain philosophical and ethical consequences, as we will explore in the next two chapters. What we have yet to learn is the place of the humanities in the shared public framework that is created when we choose to be placed. We will explore the role of the humanities toward the end of chapter 4.

2

ETHICS, ECONOMICS, AND PLACE

Space and Place:
The Ethical Importance of Understanding Where We Are

CHOOSING TO RETURN HOME and set down roots forces us to spend time with our surroundings and, if we allow ourselves, to see them not merely with a utilitarian imagination or as meaningless scenery, but with a sacramental imagination. In other words, when we see our surroundings not as stuff to please us but let ourselves see their intrinsic value instead, we create the opportunity to see our surroundings as sacramental pointers to goodness outside of our interests and ourselves. Seeing things sacramentally, therefore, has the potential to transform our values. Specifically, this new placed perspective informs our ethics and, as an extension, economics. This is no less true for Chesterton and Lewis than it is for Berry. They all wrote extensively about ethical and economic concerns, and their interest can be seen as a working-out of their rooted lives.

As at least one interviewer, Anne Husted Burleigh, has noted, Berry has an "Aristotelian-Thomistic view of the world."[1] By this she means "a world that [Berry] sees as a created order for which the Creator has appointed us stewards and trustees."[2] The base model for this view is the Great Chain of Being, which Berry discusses in his essay "Poetry and Place." In

---

1. Burleigh, "Wendell Berry," 135.
2. Ibid.

this essay, Berry contrasts classical poets like Pope, who held that humans needed to stay within their place in the created order, with Romantic poets like Shelley, who privileged the poet's ability to filter everything through his or her mind, essentially separating humans and their ability to think from everything else that can be perceived or imagined. For example, in response to Wordsworth, Berry states: "The disembodied individual mind is seen as occupying the space or perhaps the difference between the extremes of private conscience and supreme intelligence, also disembodied. The mind is not only individual here, but solitary; this difference or middle space is both natureless and cultureless."[3] A natureless and cultureless solitary human being is anti-teleological. That is, such a human being is not defined by a particular purpose or goal. According to Berry, this concept of the "disembodied individual mind" was enormously influential on our own modern views concerning humans and their environment. His views seem to coincide with those of Taylor, though Taylor sees the roots extending further back. A well-designed humanities curriculum, including these authors, will go a long way towards reducing the number of natureless, cultureless, and anti-teleological human beings.

In *Sources of the Self*, Taylor states, "The subject of disengagement and rational control has become a familiar modern figure . . . As it develops to its full form through Locke and the Enlightenment thinkers he influenced, it becomes what I want to call the 'punctual' self."[4] "The key to this figure," says Taylor, "is that it gains control through disengagement . . . always correlative of an 'objectification.'"[5] Taylor then argues Locke's influence on the creation of the modern "self," whereby we are able to, within our first-person perspective, think about ourselves in the third-person, separate from all other matter around us. In other words, we make our "selves" into its own distinct category, giving us "instrumental control," through science, over the earth.[6] This creates for moderns a paradox: "Radical objectivity is only intelligible and accessible through radical subjectivity," as Taylor points out many contemporary thinkers have said.[7] Ultimately, then, "It is a self defined by the powers of disengaged reason—with its associated ideals of self-responsible freedom and dignity—of self-exploration, and

---

3. Berry, "Poetry and Place," 186.
4. Taylor, *Sources of the Self*, 160.
5. Ibid.
6. Ibid., 161.
7. Ibid., 176.

of personal commitment."[8] Taylor's definition of the punctual self shares similarities with Hannah Arendt's discussion of the Archimedian point and is one explanation of how our modern conception of self has become essentially rootless, divorced from a communal place.[9]

In contrast, Berry's view is that humans must see themselves as part of a created order. As Burleigh stated above, this view is Aristotelean-Thomist and helps us see how Berry arrives at seeing humans as "stewards" and "trustees." Coinciding with this ordered view is Berry's emphasis on "goods." For Berry, one way we can define "good" is things achieving their purposes. In his essay "Two Economies," he contrasts our modern industrial economy with what he terms the Great Economy (loosely based on the Kingdom of God and other religious traditions). He states, "When the virtues are rightly practiced within the Great Economy, we do not call them virtues; we call them good farming, good forestry, good carpentry, good husbandry, good weaving and sewing, good homemaking, good parenthood, good neighborhood, and so on."[10] This concept of what is good, tied to the idea of a thing's proper purpose, is very similar to Alasdair MacIntyre's philosophy of internal goods, drawn as well from Aristotle. MacIntyre believes:

> [M]oral arguments within the classical, Aristotelean tradition—whether in its Greek or its medieval versions—involve at least one central functioning concept, the concept of *man* understood as having an essential nature and an essential purpose or function... That is to say, 'man' stands to 'good man' as 'watch' stands to 'good watch' or 'farmer' to 'good farmer' within the classical tradition. Aristotle takes it as a starting-point for ethical enquiry that the relationship of 'man' to 'living well' is analogous to that of 'harpist' to 'playing the harp well' (*Nichomachean Ethics*, 1095a 16).[11]

Goodness in people and things implies that there is some *telos* for those things. In other words, people and things have ideal purposes, ends—*teloi*—to strive towards and doing so makes them "good." With respect to predicating "good" of anything, MacIntyre—following Aristotle—believes, "Human beings, like members of all other species, have a specific nature; and that nature is such that they have certain aims and goals, such that

---

8. Ibid., 211.
9. Arendt, *Human Condition*, 257–68.
10. Berry, "Two Economies," 135.
11. MacIntyre, *After Virtue*, 58.

they move by nature towards a specific *telos*."¹² Aristotle called the *telos* of humans *eudaimonia*, which can be roughly translated as "blessedness, happiness, [and/or] prosperity."¹³ Not all humans start out on the same footing: some are more equipped from birth towards reaching this *telos* than others, and a system, virtues, are therefore needed to help. So virtues, for Berry, MacIntyre, and Aristotle, are those qualities that help us achieve our purposes and make us good. As MacIntyre puts it, "The virtues are precisely those qualities the possession of which will enable an individual to achieve *eudaimonia* and the lack of which will frustrate his movement toward that *telos*."¹⁴

For Berry, this movement towards the *telos* affects more than just humans or other animals; the land and communities also have a *telos* that can either be approached through an awareness and correct relationship between humans and their environment or discouraged through wrong modes of thinking and living. As he says in one interview, "The standard is the health of the community."¹⁵ The natural world can operate on its own, distinct from humans, moving towards a collective *telos*. Human beings, as rational creatures, are unique in their ability to choose whether to move towards or away from their *telos*. Also, the choices humans make can help or hinder the natural world's movement towards a *telos*. For Berry, this means that a primary working out of the *telos* of humans manifests itself in their work and "the necessary work of the world . . . [is t]o take what we've got and make it better."¹⁶

In this sense, Berry's vision for healthy communities resembles a communal/patriotic community, rather than an atomistic/welfarism¹⁷ community, to use Charles Taylor's contrasting terms.¹⁸ Taylor makes a distinction between "common" and "convergent" goods, where common goods are goods that are shared, while convergent goods are goods that we

12. Ibid., 148.

13. Ibid.

14. Ibid. One way we might view the works of these authors is to see them as enactments of virtues or critiques of virtuous actions.

15. Pennington, "Interview," 41.

16. Smith, "Field Observations," 92.

17. Taylor, *Philosophical*, 127. According to Taylor, "welfarism" is Amartya Sen's term that means, "The judgement of the relative goodness of alternative states of affairs must be based exclusively on, and taken as an increasing function of, the respective collections of individual utilities in these states."

18. Ibid., 188.

all have, but don't share.[19] An example of a common good would be friendship, while an example of a convergent good would be a fire department. We share friendship in a personal space in a way much differently from how we share a fire department that is there to help us individually in an impersonal way. Common goods have a shared language that is unique to individual communities. Taylor claims, republics "are animated by a sense of a shared immediate common good. To that degree, the bond resembles that of friendship, as Aristotle saw [in *Nicomachean Ethics*]."[20] He continues:

> The citizen is attached to the law as the repository of his and others' dignity. That might sound like the way I'm indebted to the Montreal Urban Community for its police service. But the crucial difference is that the police relationship secures what we all understand as a merely convergent good, whereas the identification of the citizen with the republic as a common enterprise is essentially the recognition of a common good. My attachment to the MUC for its police service is based on enlightened self-interest. My (frequently inoperative) moral commitment to the welfare of all humans is altruistic. But the bond of solidarity with my compatriots in a functioning republic is based on a sense of shared fate, where the sharing itself is of value. This is what gives this bond its special importance, what makes my ties with these people and to this enterprise peculiarly binding, what animates my "vertu" or patriotism.[21]

Therefore, says Taylor, "patriotism involves more than converging moral principles; it is a common allegiance to a particular historical community. [It involves] a love of the particular."[22] Of course, one of the main ways citizens can understand and share this love for a particular historic community is through the teachings of the humanities. Our literature can help us remember and learn from our shared tradition, what Chesterton calls "the democracy of the dead."[23] Then we may see ourselves not only as individuals trying to live out our own version of the American (or Western) dream, but also recognize a particular, shared common good.

This link between patriotism and love for the particular is a theme that can be clearly seen in much of Chesterton's writings, even from the earliest.

19. Ibid., 190.
20. Ibid., 191.
21. Ibid., 191–92.
22. Ibid., 198.
23. Chesterton, *Orthodoxy*, 64.

The essay "A Defence of Patriotism," reprinted in the 1902 collection of his essays, *The Defendant*, is possibly the most-often cited with regards to his views supporting local, small communities. This essay contains the oft-quoted statement, "'My country, right or wrong,' is a thing that no patriot would think of saying except in a desperate case. It is like saying, 'My mother, drunk or sober.'"[24] This well-known quip expresses a belief shared by both Chesterton and Berry: we will only really want to change the things that we love. This is why the love for particular things is so important, because without these deep attachments, there will be no true impetus to improve them. That both Chesterton and Berry despise the term "progress" when it is applied in the abstract is no surprise, because progress can only occur in the particular; we must care enough about a particular something to want to improve it and we must also have some notion of an ideal for the progress to achieve. In *Orthodoxy*, Chesterton states, "This adds a further principle to our previous list of principles. We have said we must be fond of this world, even in order to change it. We must now add that we must be fond of another world (real or imaginary) in order to have something to change it to."[25] A teleological view of the world is crucial, therefore, because it provides an ideal against which our progress can be measured as we, in Berry's terms, do "the necessary work of the world" which is "[t]o take what we've got and make it better."[26] An overarching purpose, like a return to orthodoxy, seems to be necessary for progress.

Chesterton further emphasizes the important connection between love and patriotism when he continues, "What we really need for the frustration and overthrow of a deaf and raucous Jingoism is a renascence of the love of the native land."[27] He argues (like Taylor) that the reason true patriotism can only be felt towards our local environments is because we have a connection to them, not only in our particular place and time, but extending back into tradition: "We fall back upon gross and frivolous things for our patriotism, for a simple reason. We [the English] are the only people in the world who are not taught in childhood our own literature and our own history."[28] Taylor states:

24. Chesterton, *Defendant*, 125.
25. Chesterton, *Orthodoxy*, 156.
26. Smith, "Field Observations," 92.
27. Chesterton, *Defendant*, 126.
28. Ibid., 128. Though Chesterton was primarily referring to being taught a national history, his insight should also be applied on an even more local level. How would our

> Patriotism is somewhere between friendship or family feeling, on one side, and altruistic dedication on the other. The latter has no concern for the particular: I'm inclined to act for the good of anyone anywhere. The former attaches me to particular people. My patriotic allegiance doesn't bind me to individual people in this familial way; I may not know most of my compatriots, and may not particularly want them as friends when I do meet them. But particularity enters in because my bond to these people passes through our participation in a common political entity. Functioning republics are like families in this crucial respect, that part of what binds them together is their common history.[29]

Failing to educate citizens about their shared history as part of a nation, state, or local community undermines patriotism because it neglects the particular places and events that bind a people together in a shared *telos*. Granted, this shared history may be debatable and indeed such debates need to take place. A past that is not reflected upon can introduce its own set of problems. What concerns us here are citizens divorced from *any* past, and thus unable to share any history with each other. In other words, both Chesterton and Taylor see the importance of teleology on philosophical, religious, and political levels.

Another early essay in which Chesterton works out his views of the importance of place is "The Patriotic Idea," from 1904. In it, Chesterton elaborates in much more depth some of his earlier ideas in pieces such as "A Defence of Patriotism." Throughout this piece, Chesterton defends the local place against the imperialistic cosmopolitanism of his modern age. He states, "The truth is, of course, that real universality is to be reached rather by convincing ourselves that we are in the best possible relation with our immediate surroundings."[30] Doing so, he says, makes us more human and have true love for other humans and the natural world. This is because, "The fundamental spiritual advantage of patriotism and such sentiment is this: that by means of it all things are loved adequately, because all things are loved individually."[31] Such love enables a tradition to be established,

---

citizens see themselves and each other differently if in their education (especially in the humanities) they were taught to understand their local history and culture instead of only the history and culture of such foreign (for most) places as New York City, London, Paris, or even Hollywood?

29. Taylor, *Philosophical*, 188.
30. Chesterton, "Patriotic Idea," 227.
31. Ibid.

a tradition that could only exist because it is rooted in particular things. Chesterton continues, "To the cosmopolitan, therefore, who professes to love humanity and hate local preference, we shall reply: 'How can you love humanity and hate anything so human?'"[32]

One novel of Chesterton's that works out these themes is *The Flying Inn* (1914). In it, Chesterton emphasizes the importance of place to memory/tradition in humans and also his orthodox teleology that differs from the modern technocratic utilitarianism of his age. The novel's tension centers on contradictory views of the human highest good. Chesterton's novel concerns a member of Parliament who is intent on closing every public inn in England by taking away their rights to sell liquor. Chesterton sides with the rights of the English countrymen, who are able to evade the authorities because of their particular knowledge of the countryside. They revolt against a law that denies them the pleasures of pubs because this denies them one possible way to achieve *eudaimonia*, which is to live and fare well.[33] Throughout the novel, Chesterton emphasizes a love for local places and traditions that we will examine further in the next chapter.

Besides emphasizing love of the local in each particular human's story, Chesterton also discusses what he feels is the historical story for humanity in *The Everlasting Man*. The teleology inherent in Chesterton's reading of history is that Christianity was the fulfillment of paganism. One of the first assumptions about history that Chesterton overturns is the belief that civilization replaced barbarism: "According to the real records available, barbarism and civilization were not successive states in the progress of the world. They were conditions that existed side by side, as they still exist side by side."[34] This is the "chronological snobbery" that Lewis is cured of in *Surprised by Joy*.[35] For Chesterton, therefore, there is no story of Progress for humans. He states:

> One of the ablest agnostics of the age once asked me whether I thought mankind grew better or grew worse or remained the same . . . I asked him whether he thought that Mr. Smith of Golder's Green got better or worse or remained exactly the same between the age of thirty and forty. It then seemed to dawn on him that it would rather depend on Mr. Smith; and how he chose to go on. It

32. Ibid., 229.
33. Aristotle, *Nicomachean*, 1095a19.
34. Chesterton, *Everlasting Man*, 62.
35. Lewis, *Surprised*, 207.

> had never occurred to him that it might depend on how mankind chose to go on; and that its course was not a straight line or an upward or downward curve, but a track like that of a man across a valley, going where he liked and stopping where he chose, going to church or falling drunk in a ditch. The life of man is a story; an adventure story; and in our vision the same is true even of the story of God.[36]

This relationship between the story of humanity and the story of God is what makes Christianity, for Chesterton, the necessary rival of Paganism. Chesterton continues, "The Catholic faith is the reconciliation because it is the realization both of mythology and philosophy. It is a story . . . It is a philosophy . . . But above all, it is a reconciliation because it is something that can only be called the philosophy of stories."[37] In other words, Christianity appeals to Chesterton because it simultaneously encourages humans to live good individual stories and invites them into a larger, communal story.

Similarly, Lewis deals with these issues of humans, their *telos*, ethics, and community in his writing. As discussed earlier, Chesterton's writings, especially *The Everlasting Man*, were a significant influence on Lewis's conversion to Christianity. In *Surprised By Joy*, Lewis explains that he was trying to reconcile paganism with Christianity.[38] After reading *The Everlasting Man* he "for the first time saw the whole Christian outline of history set out in a form that seemed to . . . make sense."[39] He states, "The question was no longer to find the one simply true religion among a thousand religions simply false. It was rather, 'Where has religion reached its true maturity? Where, if anywhere, have the hints of all Paganism been fulfilled?'"[40] We might define "maturity" by using the "three axes" of "moral thinking" that Taylor defines: "our sense of respect for and obligations to others, . . . our understanding of what makes a full life . . . [and] the range of notions concerned with dignity."[41] Lewis eventually agreed, of course, that the answer is Christianity.

---

36. Chesterton, *Everlasting Man*, 245–46.

37. Ibid., 246. Chesterton's point has further bearing on the humanities because much of literature teaches in the mode of narrative.

38. Lewis, *Surprised*, 235–36.

39. Ibid., 223.

40. Ibid., 235.

41. Taylor, *Sources of the Self*, 15.

Lewis's fiction also speaks to these issues. In *The Pilgrim's Regress* the hermit History tells John a narrative of history that clearly sets forth Lewis's teleological belief that Christianity is the bridge between the historical progressions of both the Gentiles and the Jews. Likewise, Lewis wrestles with differing teleological philosophies in his Space Trilogy, which consists of *Out of the Silent Planet*, *Perelandra*, and *That Hideous Strength*. We will more closely examine these issues in these novels in chapter 3. Before we look at them, however, we should first explore the intersections of orthodoxy and ethics in Lewis's philosophy at the time that he wrote them.

Contemporaneous with the *Space Trilogy* is Lewis's philosophical work *The Abolition of Man*, first published in 1944. The book is a collection of three lectures he delivered. The first lecture and the impetus behind Lewis's writing are his concerns with a current and popular English rhetoric book, *The Control of Language: A Critical Approach to Reading and Writing* (1940), by Alex King and Martin Ketley.[42] He disguises the authors' identities by referring to them as Gaius and Titius, authors of *The Green Book*. Lewis's contention with the authors is their assertion that when people make value claims, people are really making claims about their feelings. For example, the person who says, "This is sublime" really means, "I have sublime feelings."[43] Lewis asserts that this removal of an objective property to a subjective feeling is false and has dangerous consequences in how students are taught. He states, "For every one pupil who needs to be guarded from a weak excess of sensibility there are three who need to be awakened from the slumber of cold vulgarity. The task of the modern educator is not to cut down jungles but to irrigate deserts. The right defence against false sentiments is to inculcate just sentiments."[44] This discussion of an English textbook leads to a much larger discussion of ethics in parts two and three, where Lewis asserts the importance of an objective truth behind all of our value judgments that, if ignored, will lead to a powerful minority in control of a willing majority. Of course looming over the whole discussion is World War Two and the problem of fascism but, as we will see, Lewis views fascism as a symptom of a larger modern ethical problem.

For Lewis, there exists such a thing as an absolute ethical standard transhistorically held by humans, regardless of their civilizations and

---

42. Sayer, *Jack*, 252.

43. Lewis, *Abolition*, 3, italics removed.

44. Ibid., 14. Lewis is using the term "sentiments" in the stronger sense that Taylor, *Sources of the Self*, 248, relates to Shaftesbury and eighteenth century philosophy.

religions.⁴⁵ Some names given to this standard include "Natural Law or Traditional Morality or the First Principles of Practical Reason or the First Platitudes."⁴⁶ However, to simplify the discussion, Lewis chooses the *Tao* as his term for this universal morality. Lewis states, "This thing which I have called for convenience the *Tao* . . . is not one among a series of possible systems of value. It is the sole source of all value judgements. If it is rejected, all value is rejected. If any value is retained, it is retained."⁴⁷ He continues, "What purport to be new systems or (as they now call them) 'ideologies', all consist of fragments from the *Tao* itself, arbitrarily wrenched from their context in the whole and then swollen to madness in their isolation, yet still owing to the *Tao* and to it alone such validity as they possess."⁴⁸ This "swollen to madness in their isolation" that Lewis attributes to the "fragments" of the *Tao* is very similar to Taylor's concept of "hypergoods," discussed above. Both Lewis and Taylor see that if a shared public ethical framework is rejected, the fragments of the ethics that remain will be promoted to the exclusion of others. These resulting hypergoods then compete with one another, because they are divorced from the original framework that made sense of them and kept them from overstepping their boundaries.

Thus debates will arise about whose hypergoods, or "swollen fragments" should be central to our lives and issues of control will be inevitable. Lewis states, "A dogmatic belief in objective value is necessary to the very idea of a rule which is not tyranny or an obedience which is not slavery."⁴⁹ He continues, "The process which, if not checked, will abolish Man goes on apace among Communists and Democrats no less than among Fascists."⁵⁰ Lewis states: "The belief that we can invent 'ideologies' at pleasure, and the consequent treatment of mankind as mere ὕλη, specimens, preparations, begins to affect our very language. Once we killed bad men: now we liquidate unsocial elements."⁵¹ The metaphor Lewis uses to best describe the modern scientist is that of a magician. He states, "If we compare the chief

---

45. For Taylor, *Sources of the Self*, 21, this shared ethical standard stems from Plato: "Plato's distinction stands at the head of a large family of views which see the good life as a mastery of self which consists in the dominance of reason over desire."

46. Lewis, *Abolition*, 43.

47. Ibid.

48. Ibid., 43–44.

49. Ibid., 73.

50. Ibid.

51. Ibid., 74.

trumpeter of the new era (Bacon) with Marlowe's Faustus, the similarity is striking... [Bacon] rejects magic because it does not work; but his goal is that of the magician."[52] In contrast, for Lewis a re-imagined Natural Philosophy would be different: "When it explained it would not explain away. When it spoke of the parts it would remember the whole. While studying the *It* it would not lose what Martin Buber calls the *Thou*-situation."[53]

Many of the institutional/societal problems we struggle with as moderns stem from a rejection of traditional orthodoxy in favor of competing "hypergoods." These modern issues can be seen as tangible examples when we look at Lewis's fiction in the next chapter. Certainly we would expect these concerns to be prevalent in the *Space Trilogy*, written at the same time these lectures were given. Interestingly, though, Lewis returns to these issues throughout the *Chronicles of Narnia*, written a decade later. Before we look to Lewis's works, let us examine a community that shares a common public framework by turning again to Berry.

Perhaps we can best see the link between humans, their *telos*, ethics, and community through an examination of the community Berry seems most to admire: the Amish. Berry recognizes that his admiration of the Amish leaves him vulnerable to the charge of being a Luddite. In fact, he embraces this term: "I am indeed a Luddite, if by that I may mean that I would not willingly see my community—to the extent that I still have one—destroyed by any technological innovation."[54] According to Berry, the Amish act regardless of who is their neighbor—they treat their neighbors with respect and provide them with help based on the fact that they are neighbors. Also, they do not seek to buy out their neighbors to enlarge their own farms, but respect them and see the importance of a connected group of neighbors that share in the fate of the larger community. This respect and privileging of community can perhaps be seen most clearly in the resistance of the Amish to most forms of modern technology. As Berry has stated several times, the primary question the Amish asked when faced with a new technology is, "What will this do to our community?"

According to Donald Kraybill and Marc Olshan in *The Amish Struggle with Modernity*, "[T]he Amish are engaged in a war against the spirit of progress—against arrogance, against progress as a goal, and against the

---

52. Ibid., 77–78.
53. Ibid., 79.
54. Berry, "Simple," 58.

social fragmentation and alienation that often accompanies some forms of 'progress.'"[55] They continue:

> Their battle has been against a particular concept of progress—one that has been enthusiastically embraced by much of the rest of the world since the Enlightenment. This notion of progress rests on the perfectibility of human institutions. It is founded on the confidence that reason and its handmaiden, technology, will eventually eradicate war, hunger, poverty, and all other evils that plague human beings. For the Amish such a view of progress is only one more expression of arrogance.[56]

In modern culture, this "arrogance" often goes hand in hand with rugged individualism. In contrast, "the Amish argue that genuine satisfaction comes not from an unbridled individualism but from giving oneself up in service of an orderly community."[57] Above all, they see pride as the enemy of community.[58]

Due to these beliefs, one of the key issues the Amish have continuously and consistently faced is if and how to implement new technologies into their communities. To other Americans, implementing time and labor-saving devices may seem like a no-brainer. In fact, advertisers constantly convince consumers that these two factors outweigh all others to the extent that they, combined with the term "new," are perhaps the three most touted criteria by which new technologies are sold. In contrast, states Jameson Wetmore, "Like many scholars of technology, the Amish have rejected the idea that technologies are value-free tools. Instead, they recognize that technology and social order are constructed simultaneously and influence each other a great deal."[59] One member of the Amish community put the matter this way, "Machinery is not wrong in itself, but if it doesn't help fellowship you shouldn't have it."[60] The Amish are thus willing to accept limits to the technology that they use in order to protect their communities.

Of course, this acceptance of limits runs directly counter to the norms of modern society. According to Arendt, one consequence of scientific technology is that the "industrial revolution has replaced all workmanship

---

55. Kraybill and Olshan, *Amish Struggle*, vii.
56. Ibid.
57. Kraybill, "Introduction," 7.
58. Ibid.
59. Whetmore, "Amish Technology," 298.
60. Ibid., 300.

with labor, and the result has been that the things of the modern world have become labor products whose natural fate is to be consumed, instead of work products which are there to be used."[61] Another consequence is a heavy reliance of humans on machines, about which she states, "The question therefore is not so much whether we are the masters or the slaves of our machines, but whether machines still serve the world and its things, or if, on the contrary, they and the automatic motion of their processes have begun to rule and even destroy world and things."[62] Thus, "[f]or a society of laborers, the world of machines has become a substitute for the real world, even though this pseudo world cannot fulfil the most important task of human artifice, which is to offer mortals a dwelling place more permanent and more stable than themselves."[63] So for Berry and the Amish, as for Arendt, places should be valued more than technology and be seen as more permanent, outlasting those who dwell in them. In order to privilege places in such a worldview, humans must recognize that technology—by its very nature quickly obsolete and meant to be used up and discarded—is categorically opposed to permanence. If used unreflectively, therefore, technology will use up, rather than improve, places.

Besides his comments in essays and interviews, Berry explores the ethical philosophy of the Amish that resists technology and limitless expansion in his fiction, particularly the short novel *Remembering*. This novel follows the story of Andy Catlett, a resident of Port William, Kentucky. Andy grows up in Port William, the son of a farmer. When he is old enough he goes off to college and, after earning his degree, marries and moves to San Francisco to become a journalist. After a short time there he moves to Chicago to become a writer for the journal *Scientific Farming*, whose editor is an old high school friend named Tommy Netherbough. However, Andy becomes restless and, seeing the destructive ways of agribusiness, refuses to write a story about a modern farmer and consequently loses his job. He returns to Port William to farm in between speaking engagements at conferences, where he is called to represent the unpopular position of traditional farming. While harvesting corn in his community, Andy loses his hand to a corn picker. This trauma causes him to become angry with his wife and his children and so, while on a trip to speak at a college in San Francisco, he skips his commitment to speak and checks into a hotel, where he wrestles

61. Arendt, *Human Condition*, 124.
62. Ibid., 151.
63. Ibid., 152.

with his injury and his memories, trying to decide whether to return to his family or not. After taking an early morning walk through the city to the coast and reflecting on various memories of his family and community, he returns home.

In *Remembering*, Berry contrasts the ethical philosophy of agribusiness with the Amish method of farming when Andy is sent by his editor at *Scientific Farming* to Ohio to interview Bill Meikelberger, the magazine's Premier Farmer for that year. After interviewing Meikelberger, Andy travels to Pittsburgh, but on the way his attention is caught by an Amish farmer, Isaac Troyer, whom he sees plowing in a field. Andy stops and spends much of the day with Isaac, doing an informal interview. Andy is drawn to the Amish way of life and decides to write his article on Troyer instead of Meikelberger, thus leading to the confrontation with his editor that costs him his job.

In the span of a few pages, Berry lays out two contrasting ways of farming, that of Meikelberger and that of Troyer. Examining their differences can help illuminate some of the key aspects of Amish life that Berry so admires. Meikelberger sought to escape the limits placed upon him by the farm he inherited from his parents. In contrast, Troyer accepted and respected the limits his farm placed upon him. The differing philosophies of the farmers can be seen in three categories: isolation versus community, sterility versus virility, and poverty versus wealth.

First, Meikelberger buys out his neighbors' farms, while Troyer respects his neighbors and accepts limits on what he can reasonably farm himself. In consequence, Meikelberger relies on a "herd of machines," while Troyer uses animals that he breeds himself.[64] These points are not mutually exclusive: Meikelberger's decision to enlarge his own farm by buying out his neighbors forced him to have to adopt technology and replace his animals with machines in order to farm the additional ground by himself. Meikelberger has therefore clearly chosen to isolate his family, both by eliminating his immediate neighbors and by using machines instead of hiring workers and animals to share in the work on his farm. By doing so he has adopted a system that is consequentially not renewable: his machines will not reproduce and, in order to run, must consume fossil fuels that do not come from the farm. In contrast, Troyer's farm is much more self-sufficient, while also less isolated because of its proximity to neighbors and therefore community.

64. Berry, *Remembering*, 180.

Second, Meikelberger has a sterile, empty house and fields, while Troyer's house and fields are full of the life of his family, including his livestock. Because of the ever-increasing overhead to upkeep technology on the farm and to pay debts, Meikelberger's wife must go into town to work a second job, while Troyer's wife can stay at home and participate in the life of the farm. Also, the technology of the farm has eliminated roles for Meikelberger's children, so they have gone to college and moved away, while Troyer's children will (probably) continue in the life of the farm and inherit it one day. These contrasting points further emphasize the sterility of Meikelberger's farm in contrast to Troyer's.

Third, because of the ever-increasing debt to upkeep machines and maintain a large agribusiness, Meikelberger stays busy all of the time between working and fighting off creditors, while Troyer and his family rest on Sundays and after dinner each day. In contrast, Meikelberger is very much in debt, while Troyer nets "about half" in an average year.[65] This means that after Troyer subtracts his expenses from his gross (or total) profit, he is left with approximately half of his gross profit each year. In consequence, Meikelberger's stress and worrying have given him an ulcer, while Troyer appears to be healthy and vibrant. Finally, we are told that "Meikelberger's ambition had made common cause with a technical power that proposed no limit to itself, that was, in fact, destroying Meikelberger, as it had already destroyed nearly all that was natural or human around him."[66] In stark contrast, when Andy tells Troyer he hopes they will "meet again," Troyer replies, "I'll be here," and we believe him because he does not have debt and his farm is very much alive.[67]

Here we can clearly see the ethical consequences that result from one's relationship with a place—whether that place is seen as something to be escaped and exploited or to be accepted and respected. Both Meikelberger and Troyer wanted to achieve *eudaimonia* for their families, but their belief about the places in which they lived and consequently how they farmed those places brought about very different ends. Ironically, Meikelberger pursued wealth to achieve *eudaimonia* for his family but has lost his family from his farm and is in debt. Troyer, on the other hand, made the health of his place his standard and as a consequence is debt free and has a net

---

65. Ibid., 187.
66. Ibid., 182.
67. Ibid., 188.

profit of about half. The relationship between place, ethics, and economy is therefore very closely connected, as we will see in the next section.

Recovering the Meaning of Economy

Today, when we hear the term "the economy," we likely think about an abstract superstructure that encompasses the relationship between consumers and businesses, made concrete by representation in dollar amounts. However, this particularly modern definition of "economy" is not the only definition, but has replaced an older, classical definition. In essence, there are two key differing understandings of "economy." The Greek word for economy is "oikonomia," which refers to the management of households. This is because the ancients separated households from political life and relegated economic dealings with this private sphere of life, while politics were in the public sphere. Aristotle separated the art of household management from the art of getting wealth: "Now it is easy to see that the art of household management is not identical with the art of getting wealth, for the one uses the material which the other provides."[68] Aristotle clearly separates the two economic goals:

> Hence some persons are led to believe that getting wealth is the object of household management, and the whole idea of their lives is that they ought either to increase their money without limit, or at any rate not to lose it. The origin of this disposition in men is that they are intent upon living only, and not upon living well; and, as their desires are unlimited, they also desire that the means of gratifying them should be without limit. Those who do aim at a good life seek the means of obtaining bodily pleasures; and, since the enjoyment of these appears to depend on property, they are absorbed in getting wealth: and so there arises the second species of wealth-getting. For, as their enjoyment is in excess, they seek an art which produces the excess of enjoyment; and, if they are not able to supply their pleasures by the art of getting wealth, they try other causes, using in turn every faculty in a manner contrary to nature.[69]

Of the two, Aristotle privileged living well over merely living. Humans need to work in order to provide a living, but once that living has been

---

68. Aristotle, *Politics*, 1256a1–1256b25.
69. Ibid., 1257b18–1258a14.

obtained, they are free, in Aristotle's thinking, to engage in the public realm. However, some humans continue to pursue wealth-getting, or making a living, even after their basic needs are met. Arendt states, "If the property-owner chose to enlarge his property instead of using it up in leading a political life, it was as though he willingly sacrificed his freedom and became voluntarily what the slave was against his own will, a servant of necessity."[70] For Aristotle, the worst form of rejecting freedom was found in usury:

> There are two sorts of wealth-getting, as I have said; one is a part of household management, the other is retail trade: the former is necessary and honourable, while that which consists in exchange is justly censured; for it is unnatural, and a mode by which men gain from one another. The most hated sort, and with the greatest reason, is usury, which makes a gain out of money itself, and not from the natural object of it.[71] For money was intended to be used in exchange, but not to increase at interest. And this term interest, which means the birth of money from money, is applied to the breeding of money because the offspring resembles the parent. That is why of all modes of getting wealth this is the most unnatural.[72]

Clearly, for Aristotle usury was the most unethical form of securing *eudaimonia*, because it most violated the *telos* of money: it no longer was a direct representative for a natural object, securing private needs to free oneself for public life, but was made to unnaturally make more money. This aversion to usury and the original definition of "economy" seem to have been kept throughout the Middle Ages.[73]

Of course, this aversion did not last, as our modern understanding of "economy" is largely built upon usury: trading stocks to use money to make more money. According to the *Oxford English Dictionary*, the usage "the economy" first occurred in 1892, after the Industrial Revolution had firmly

---

70. Arendt, *Human Condition*, 65.

71. One needs only think of the recent collapse of the banking industry, caused by the unregulated "usury" of profit gains that had no correlation to reality.

72. Aristotle, *Politics*, 1258a39–1258b8.

73. *Oxford English Dictionary*, 3rd ed., s.v. "economy." I realize this view of usury is radical today. Today we acquiesce to a banking system built on making money from our debt, so much so that we protect and exempt it from punishment when it errs. Also, perhaps the best modern example of money's symbolic power is our national debt—we use it in argument to sway each other to political sides, but none of us has actually seen this debt. In other words, its only reality to us is as symbol, albeit a powerful and persuasive one.

changed the economic structure of society. This has become the common usage of today, putting the emphasis on a collective national or supranational economy rather than the management of the individual households/communities that make them up. Today, we see this economy existing in two primary forms: socialism, where a centralized government controls the market exchange system and distributes wealth amongst its citizens; and, more commonly, capitalism, where a centralized government steps aside (theoretically) to let its citizens distribute wealth amongst themselves in a free-market, survival of the fittest, economy.

This modern economy of free-market capitalism has not been without its detractors, one of whom was Marx in the 1840s. But starting in the 1890s, in response to worldwide "unchecked competition," "rapacious usury," and the mistreatment of workers as "slave[s]," and the growing gap between the upper and lower classes, Pope Leo XIII issued the encyclical *Rerum Novarum*.[74] *Rerum Novarum* was a refutation of socialism that tried to eliminate private property by preying on the lower classes' "envy" of the upper classes.[75] Instead, the Pope claimed "every man has by nature the right to possess property as his own."[76] As such, *Rerum Novarum* was a criticism of both extreme free-market capitalism and socialism, because both extremes removed the possession of private property from the many to the few. In other words, the rich get richer and the poor get poorer. Building on this Catholic encyclical, in 1926 the Distributist League was founded by Chesterton. Primarily English and Catholic, the members sought to promote a third option to the too-similar communism and extreme capitalism.[77] The league included such writers as Hilaire Belloc, Arthur J. Penty, and Fr. Vincent McNabb. In the midst of the rapidly changing modern world, their voices were almost completely forgotten by the middle of the twentieth century. Perhaps their fizzling out is not without warrant—post-WWII was like a shot of adrenaline to industrial capitalism and the Distributists understandably appeared anachronistic, if not utopian and fanciful. Only recently have their works begun to be reprinted and their ideas discussed.[78]

74. *Rerum Novarum*, par. 3.
75. Ibid., par. 4.
76. Ibid., par. 6.
77. Naylor, "Averting Self-Destruction."
78. Also, though not usually intentionally Distributist, such increasingly popular practices like co-ops, food shares, and even eBay can be seen as derived from similar economic thought.

One such work is Arthur J. Penty's 1937 pamphlet "Distributism: A Manifesto." In it, Penty defines the purpose of Distributists as the following:

> Distributists propose to go back to fundamentals, and to rebuild society from its basis in agriculture, instead of accepting the industrial system and changing the ownership, which is all that Socialists propose. Apart from their conviction that Industrialism is essentially unstable and cannot last, Distributists refuse to accept it as a foundation upon which to build, because they believe that large-scale industry may be as great a tyranny under public as under private ownership. They therefore seek to get the smallholder back into industry as they seek to get him back onto the land; and they accept all the implications which such a revolutionary process involves.[79]

That Berry holds a similar position to this foundational belief of the Distributists is readily apparent.[80] He begins a recent essay with these words: "My economic point of view is from ground-level. It is a point of view sometimes described as 'agrarian.' That means in ordering the economy of a household or community or nation, I would put nature first, the economies of land use second, the manufacturing economy third, and the consumer economy fourth."[81] But Berry's similarities do not stop there. In a 1999 interview, Berry claims that "economic and intellectual independence . . . is founded on land ownership."[82] He continues, "Going back very far, it has to do with the belief in the importance of small ownership, the small holding. Jefferson's agrarianism certainly has to do with that and so does Virgil's . . . If you are going to take democracy seriously, there has to be a balance in favor of the small landowners."[83] Why are small landowners so important? Because, he says, "People who are economically independent can think and vote independently."[84]

Ultimately, the "implications" of getting small business owners and farmers "back onto the land" involve one form or another of limiting. The

---

79. Penty, "Distributism," 93.

80. Berry's similarity to the Distributists is important because it demonstrates that, though starting from very different historical and cultural periods, Berry and Chesterton share a belief in a return to the same orthodox tradition for the ideals underpinning their challenges to the corruptions of modern economic practice.

81. Berry, "Money," 3.

82. Burleigh, "Wendell Berry's Community," 142.

83. Ibid.

84. Ibid.

importance of limits is a prominent theme throughout Berry's essays and fiction. A close look at some of the Catholic Distributists reveals this theme as well. Although Lewis did not explicitly deal with economic issues in the same systematic ways as Chesterton and Berry, glimpses of his economic philosophy can be inferred from several places in his fiction. Greed and its coexistence with utilitarianism are both issues in the *Space Trilogy*, typified in the character or Devine/Lord Feverstone.[85] Other works that explore this relationship between greed and utilitarianism include *The Lion, the Witch, and the Wardrobe*, *The Magician's Nephew*, and *The Last Battle*. We will look at some of these examples in his Narnia stories in chapter 3. For now, we will compare the ideas of the Distributists with Wendell Berry. Though by no means exhaustive, three important limits to our economic beliefs that the Distributists and Wendell Berry seem to share include limits to technology, limits to our use of money, and limits to our selves.

First, both the Distributists and Berry view some technology as destructive to the culture of communities, and therefore feel it should be limited. Penty states in his manifesto that "Distributists would not only restrict the use of machinery where it stands in the way of widespread distribution of property, but also where it conflicts with what they are accustomed to regard as the permanent interests of life."[86] These include "the interests of society, religion, human values, art and culture" that should "come first, and that the use of machinery should be prohibited wherever it runs counter to them."[87] Likewise, in *The Outline of Sanity* Chesterton argues that humans can live without machines.[88] Recalling what Aristotle said about what constitutes the good life, he states, "There is no obligation on us to be richer, or busier, or more efficient, or more productive, or more progressive, or in any way worldlier or wealthier, if it does not make us happier."[89] It is important to note here that the Distributists were not calling for the destruction of all modern technology, but were making the point that machines should be used only when they did not undermine some greater good of the community. Similarly, in praising the type of modern community he admires most,

---

85. Oyarsa says to Weston in *Out of the Silent Planet*, 138: "He [the Bent One, or Satan] has only bent you; but this Thin One [Devine] who sits on the ground he has broken, for he has left him nothing but greed. He is now only a talking animal and in my world he could do no more evil than an animal." Here Lewis implies that greed is dehumanizing.

86. Penty, "Distributism," 94.

87. Ibid.

88. Chesterton, *Outline*, 162–66.

89. Ibid., 163.

Berry claims that "the Amish are the truest geniuses of technology, for they understand the necessity of limiting it, and they know how to limit it."[90] He explains, "By living well without such 'necessities' as automobiles, tractors, electrical power, and telephones, the Amish prove them unnecessary and so give the lie to our 'economy.'"[91] Elsewhere, he uses the entertainment industry for an example. He says that through "remembering and telling stories, singing, dancing, playing games, and even by their work" humans entertained themselves until in the last seventy-five years, where now a small selection of overpaid people do those things for others' "passive" enjoyment.[92] Communities are therefore letting technology—in such forms as television, DVDs, recorded music, the Internet—replace a valuable aspect of their culture.

Besides undermining culture, the Distributists and Berry also agree that technology helps create unemployment. For example, Fr. McNabb shows in *The Church and the Land* that while machines allow a fixed number of humans to work them, the land is flexible and can accommodate many more humans, as long as agriculture remains unmechanized.[93] Obviously, that has not remained the case post-World War II, and increased mechanization in agriculture has meant the need for fewer farmers and a large migration of farmers to the city to become part of the "permanently unemployable" that Berry laments.[94] More recently, Berry writes, "At the root of our problem . . . is industrialism and the Industrial revolution itself. As the original Luddites saw clearly and rightly, the purpose of industrialism from the first has been to replace human workers with machines."[95] As stated earlier, he claims to be a Luddite in the sense that he "would not willingly see [his] community . . . destroyed by any technological innovation."[96]

Second, both Berry and the Distributists view money as a "token" and not actual wealth. In his Manifesto, Penty claims that the problem with money is that people want to use it to make more money instead of as "a common measure of value."[97] "Thus," says Penty, "the problem of money is

---

90. Berry, *Unsettling*, 212.
91. Ibid.
92. Berry, "Money," 10.
93. McNabb, *Church*, 121.
94. Berry, "What," 106–7.
95. Berry, "Money," 19.
96. Berry, "Simple," 58.
97. Penty, "Distributism," 96.

seen to be primarily a moral issue."[98] Likewise, Fr. McNabb, in rebuking an agribusinessman, criticizes him for being "too deeply engaged in *making a fair return for capital*, that is, in making money," failing to realize that "[m]oney is not primary wealth or even secondary wealth, because it is not real wealth, but only token wealth."[99] By primary wealth, McNabb means the four essentials of food, clothing, housing, and fuel for heating and cooking, while secondary wealth includes non-essentials, such as consumer goods and transportation systems.[100] For the Distributists, the dilemmas of "property, usury, and credit" could be solved by fixing taxes, interest rates, and wages.[101] Their fixation would slowly dismantle both "the capitalist and the banking system."[102]

Berry also believes our modern view and use of money needs to be corrected. He states, "Money, instead of a token signifying the value of goods, becomes a good in itself, which the wealthy can easily manipulate in their own favor."[103] He calls us a "nation of fantasists," because we "think that shopping is a patriotic act and public service. We tolerate fabulous capitalists who think a bet on a debt is an asset."[104] Berry, like the Distributists, sees in our bank system the problem of usury, which he strongly opposes, calling it "a violence against God because it is a violence against nature."[105] This belief echoes Aristotle, who called usury the most "unnatural" way to gain wealth. Berry's solution to usury, like the Distributists' solution, is to encourage bankers to be community members. Many people today are turning to local credit unions, for example, as an alternative to the large multi-national banks that have been unpopular since their "bail-outs" by

98. Ibid.

99. McNabb, *Church*, 145.

100. Ibid., 41. It may be difficult for us as moderns to think of transportation systems as non-essential, because they are so ingrained into our daily lives, from the goods that we buy to our daily commutes. However, humans were able to live and thrive before such systems existed, by living in much more localized economies that contained the essentials now spread out by our transportation systems.

101. Penty, "Distributism," 97.

102. Ibid. These claims, of course, are radical, but nevertheless relevant today. In American politics we are currently debating the widening gap between the rich and poor, bank regulations and interest rates, and even possible tax fixation among the wealthiest.

103. Berry, "Money," 14–15.

104. Berry, "Simple," 56. Once again, the recent banking collapse comes to mind, where banks were insuring the bad loans they were issuing in order to make a profit when those loans defaulted.

105. Berry, "Money," 11.

the federal government. Local banking helps make this level of irresponsibility much more difficult to achieve. Berry states, "I don't think a fair rate can be determined according to standards that are only financial. It would have to be determined by responsible bankers, acting also as community members, in the context of their community, local nature, and the local economy."[106] This belief is similar to one Belloc proposes, when he says that co-operative banks, protected by law, may be able to protect local guilds from the banking monopoly.[107]

Responsibility does not lie solely with bankers, however. The choices we make as individuals are the third and possibly most important way we can provide healthy limits to our economy. In *The Outline of Sanity*, Chesterton admits, "We cannot pretend to be offering merely comforts and conveniences. Whatever our ultimate view of labour-saving machinery, we cannot offer our ideal as a labour-saving machine . . . There is no way out of the danger except the dangerous way."[108] Chesterton therefore makes a "call for volunteers."[109] Similarly, Belloc says the process begins by changing "an attitude of the mind."[110] Likewise, Fr. McNabb claims, "No people has ever left the town for the land, or remained on the land when it could have gone to the town, except under the motive of religion."[111] He therefore asks of his reader: "If God allows you a plot of soil, and hands for toil, why should you be solicitous to have your revenues from Babylonian brickworks— your meat from Babylonian cold-storage— your drink from Babylonian waterworks— your clothes from Babylonian cloth-factories? Is there no clay in Sussex soil— are there no cattle in Sussex meadows— is there no water in Sussex wells— is there no wool in Sussex sheep?"[112]

Amazingly, McNabb wrote these words in 1925, long before such modern conveniences as overnight transnational shipping and bottled water. What the Distributists make clear from these statements is that at the root of the economic problem are the lifestyle choices made daily by individuals. The choices often seem to hinge on two things: what is convenient in the short-term for the individual and what is inconvenient but good for

---

106. Ibid., 13.
107. Belloc, *Servile State*, 144.
108. Chesterton, *Outline*, 130–31.
109. Ibid., 133.
110. Belloc, *Servile State*, 62.
111. McNabb, *Church*, 36.
112. Ibid., 38.

the long-term health of the community. As Chesterton admitted, these choices are not easy to make. Like Chesterton, Berry also readily admits the difficulties of choosing what is best for the community in our modern culture. For instance, even though Berry's garden provides most of his vegetables and he has chosen to not own a tractor, TV, fax machine, computer, or answering machine, he does occasionally purchase some produce out of season and his diet also includes such non-local foods such as fruit, coffee, and tea.[113] Berry states, "We're not fanatics."[114] As he emphasizes elsewhere, "no community is or ever can be entirely self-sufficient."[115] So the principle of limiting seems to be one of degree, not all-or-nothing. However, both the Distributists and Berry agree that individuals must ask these questions of limit regarding their lifestyle choices, because a good economy is essential to a healthy community.

As we've seen, these authors have rejected the embrace of a post-industrial economy and called for a return to previous systems of economic living. For moderns, their conservative ideology is certainly radical, challenging deep-seated modes of thinking and operating. Certainly, their calls for a return will be unsettling to many. As we have seen, Chesterton, Lewis, and Berry called for three primary returns. First, they called for society to return to the land and communities built upon an agrarian foundation, rejecting the modern tendency to reject the country and migrate to the city.[116] Second, they called for a return to the proper use of "goods" and money, rejecting usury and the endless pursuit of money as the proper end or measure for an economy.[117] Third, they called for a return to personal ethical choices as the starting place to recover a proper and healthy economy,

---

113. Minick, "Citizen," 159–60.

114. Ibid., 159.

115. Berger, "Heaven," 176.

116. In an interview with Kate Turner, Berry says of Lewis: "The fundamental difference between [C. S. Lewis] and me . . . is probably not one of belief but one of life. He was a scholar, a man whose life was devoted almost exclusively to books. And I'm an agrarian and a farmer . . . Lewis in his time didn't *have* to think of the things we're having to think of now. The agrarian class, the agrarian tradition in England was more intact in Lewis's time than it is now" (quoted in Dickerson & O'Hara, *Narnia*, 267–68). However, I would disagree a bit with Berry, both because Lewis had to have known about the Distributists and their criticisms of modern agriculture through his love for Chesterton and also because of the respect Lewis shows for nature and farming, especially in the Narnia stories.

117. More than usury in the narrow sense, I'm using Chesterton's term to describe many features of late capitalism. Chesterton's use of the term is similar to Berry's: both are using the term polemically.

rather than looking to a centralized government and/or super-corporations to provide a top-down solution. A worldview founded on an economic philosophy like theirs leads to some important practical applications, which we will examine in their fiction in the next chapter.

3

IMPERIALISM AS ANTITHESIS TO PLACE

As we have discussed earlier, the good life, per Taylor, was classically divided into two types, the ordinary life and the contemplative/political life. The ordinary life was the prerequisite for the contemplative/political life, and the contemplative/political life was a higher "good" than the ordinary life. When this privileging gets reversed through the Protestant Reformation, then Renaissance and Enlightenment,[1] a dramatic shift in perspective occurs. When humans are engaged in contemplation and political action, they are outwardly focused, recognizing a greater community of which they are a part. In order to sustain a prolonged engagement in contemplation and political action, one must also be rooted. In contrast, when humans are concerned with the ordinary life, they are concerned with personal matters like wealth, comfort, and status. This privileging of one's ordinary life helps contribute to the detached, individualistic nature of our society. Our modern version of the "good life" states that we are all individuals seeking our own versions of the ordinary life. For many, the ordinary life amounts to a "good life" of comfort and wealth, as for instance embodied in the American Dream. As a consequence, the humanities become devalued in favor of "practical," utilitarian disciplines such as science and mathematics that have a more easily observable correlation to the industrial world of commerce and open the door to the comfort and wealth of ordinary life. Therefore, a return to the pursuit of shared corporate goods,

---

1. See Taylor, *Sources of the Self*, 211–16.

through contemplation or political action, allows one to regain a rooted ethical perspective that should be an integral part of the humanities.[2] Such an ethics allows humans to have respect for other individuals, communities, and the natural world.

By respect, I mean not a classical (heroic) or even a modern understanding as Taylor defines it. In other words, not the respect warriors earn because of the "honour ethic" or the framing of the "principle of respect . . . in terms of rights" by the "modern West."[3] Rather, it is recognition of a thing's creational goodness, possession of a *telos*, and redemptive possibility. For Chesterton, Lewis, and Berry, this ethical framework is founded in the Judeo-Christian account in Genesis, which sees Creation as good but fallen and believes the intended *telos* of everything on Earth is a restoration of relationship with the Creator. In this traditional reading of the Judeo-Christian worldview, after creating the Earth and all that is in it including humans, God called his creation "very good."[4] However, in chapter 3 of Genesis humans disobeyed God's one limitation placed upon them and as a consequence death (the consequence of sin) entered into the world. However, throughout the OT runs the message of eventual restoration. Perhaps the most famous instance of this Old Testament promise is in Isaiah:

> "For behold, I create new heavens and a new earth, and the former things shall not be remembered or come into mind . . . [N]o more shall be heard in it the sound of weeping and the cry of distress. | No more shall there be in it an infant who lives but a few days, or an old man who does not fill out his days . . . They shall build houses and inhabit them; they shall plant vineyards and eat their fruit. | They shall not plant and another eat; . . . my chosen shall long enjoy the works of their hands. They shall not labor in vain or bear children for their calamity . . . The wolf and the lamb shall graze together; the lion shall eat straw like the ox, and dust shall be the serpent's food. They shall not hurt or destroy in all my holy mountain," says the Lord.[5]

Here we see included in this promise the creation of new heavens and earth which restores things to the way they were before the Fall described in

---

2. For an extended discussion of the importance of contemplating the Good, see Murdoch, *The Sovereignty of the Good*.

3. Taylor, *Sources of the Self*, 20, 11.

4. Gen 1:31. Unless otherwise noted, all subsequent biblical quotations are taken from The Holy Bible, English Standard Version.

5. Isa 65:17–25.

Genesis: no suffering, no early death, no wasted or unpleasant labor, and peace throughout all of creation. This promised restoration continues in the New Testament. We see this clearly when John writes in Revelation:

> Then I saw a new heaven and a new earth, for the first heaven and the first earth had passed away and the sea was no more. And then I saw the holy city, new Jerusalem, coming down out of heaven from God . . . And I heard a loud voice from the throne saying, "Behold, the dwelling place of God is with man . . . He will wipe away every tear from their eyes, and death shall be no more, neither shall there be mourning, nor crying, nor pain anymore, for the former things have passed away."
>
> And he who was seated on the throne said, "Behold, I am making all things new."[6]

So we see quite clearly a teleological narrative in the Judeo-Christian tradition that ends in the restoration by God of a "very good" creation that had severed its relationship with him.

Thus, the Judeo-Christian tradition places emphasis on the restoration of relationships to God, others, and the natural order as central for humans to achieve the "good life." By "good life," I mean when things act according to their *telos* and in recognition of the "respect" of themselves and others, especially in their standing towards God. Living the good life requires seeing oneself as not just an individual, but part of a larger created order. This definition goes back to a pre-modern Christian understanding.[7] Individuals, communities, and the natural world are connected in a triangle of interdependence. This connection exists because the choices individuals make affect not only themselves, but also other human beings and the natural world. Choices communities make affect not only individuals but the natural world as well. Equally so, the natural world makes demands upon how humans live, both individually and communally. None of these three aspects of the created order functions in isolation, and to seek a good life purely in individualistic terms is not possible if it weakens the health

---

6. Rev 21:1–5.

7. For this and what follows, I differ a bit from how Taylor presents this historical shift. He shows how the Puritans returned to the Genesis account of creation as "good" and the role of humans to be "stewards," in order to assert the ordinary life and its instrumental stance towards the world as the highest good (*Sources of the Self,* 211–33). I'm arguing that Chesterton, Lewis, and Berry write out of a pre-Reformation Christianity that viewed these same texts sacramentally and thus privileged the contemplative over the ordinary life.

of one's community or natural environment, because they too are deemed "very good" and are in the process of being restored. This understanding of the good life mixes with Aristotle's understanding in the attention given to people, places, and things. Recognizing their created nature makes them sacramental pointers back to God. So contemplation and political action (how to care for creation as stewards) is once again privileged above affirmation of the individualistic ordinary life as the highest good.

Political action is therefore essential to the good life because questions must be asked about how to best affirm and/or bring about the restorative nature of created things. One key issue that must be addressed is how to move away from a utilitarian relationship to these created things, as this perspective ignores their sacredness, instead of seeing them exclusively as resources to be used up in service of some individualistic goal (such as maximizing shareholder profit, or preserving humanity for eternity). As such, a rooted ethic rejects all forms of imperialism because it is utilitarian and does not respect the essential goodness of that from which it takes. Therefore, we would expect authors who write out of a rooted ethical system would take a hard stance against imperialism as a means of achieving the "good life" for humans.

Imperialism takes many forms, one of which familiar to us is the imposing of restrictions on the lower classes by upper class policy makers. The same was true at the turn of the twentieth century, when many politicians and social scientists developed numerous reforms that changed with each new scientific or philosophical discovery. The problem with these reforms is that they were instrumental; their implementation was meant to achieve some better way to improve the ordinary life on humanity's path towards progress. As such, they neglected the sacred personhood of the individuals they were intended to help. Chesterton staunchly defended the common Englishman from what he saw as a tyranny of the intellectual upper class to chase after these philosophical fads that led to laws preventing the poor from achieving a "good life." For Chesterton, this good life included first of all the necessities of ordinary life such as home and property, access to food and ale, and stability. In *What's Wrong with the World*, Chesterton writes of the Homelessness of Jones (his everyman): "The ordinary Englishman has been duped out of his possessions, such as they were, and always in the name of progress . . . This man (Jones let us call him) has always desired the divinely ordered things; he has married for love, he has chosen or built a small house that fits like a coat; he is ready to be a great grandfather and a local god. And just as he is moving in, something goes wrong. Some tyranny, personal or political, suddenly debars him from the home . . ."[8] We see here that Chesterton is affirming the good life for English lower classes which he saw as being attacked by instrumental ways to "progress" embodied in the reforms passed by the upper "ruling" classes.

Chesterton goes on to sum up the journey Jones must make from his home to a city slum to work in a factory, all at the bidding of philosophers in the name of progress. Chesterton's gripe seems to be with the upper class's utilitarian method of instituting sweeping changes in the name of progress for all at the expense of the poor who must relinquish what little they have. This defense of the individual[9] is seen most clearly at the end of *What's Wrong with the World*, this exaggerated and polemical collection of essays, when Chesterton laments a law instituted by the upper class requiring the heads of school girls to be shaved to prevent the spread of lice, rather than changing the cause of the lice: the awful conditions in which the poor are forced to live.[10] He states:

> With the red hair of one she-urchin in the gutter I will set fire to all modern civilization. Because a girl should have long hair, she should have clean hair; because she should have clean hair, she should not have an unclean home . . . That little urchin with the gold-red hair . . . she shall not be lopped and lamed and altered; her hair shall not be cut short like a convict's . . . She is the human and sacred image; all around her the social fabric shall sway and split and fall; the pillars of society shall be shaken, and the roofs of ages come rushing down; and not one hair of her head shall be harmed.[11]

Any economic or societal change should thus be made with this respect for the good life or well being of the individual. This seems to speak strongly to Chesterton's view of the individual: above all else, humans should be valued because they are humans.

Chesterton's defense of the creational goodness inherent in individuals continued in his defense of communities, as he was always in favor of the small rather than the large. This conviction can be seen quite clearly in Chesterton's opposition to the Boer War. Standing against other powerful

---

8. Chesterton, *What's Wrong*, 58.
9. Here I am not talking about individualism, but things valued for themselves.
10. Chesterton, *What's Wrong*, 192–94.
11. Ibid., 194.

voices like H. G. Wells and G. B. Shaw, Chesterton argued against England's invasion of South Africa and said that the Boers had a right to defend their homes.[12] Chesterton fictionalized his philosophy regarding the defense of small nations in *The Napoleon of Notting Hill* (1904) and *The Flying Inn* (1914). He did not stop there, however, as he saw that the same philosophical impetus that led a nation's leadership to invade and take from another could also cause the leadership to invade and take from its own citizens. Therefore, he also tackled the problem of the imperialism of England by England in both *The Napoleon of Notting Hill* and *The Flying Inn*.

The Napoleon of Notting Hill is set in the future, 1984,[13] though it is concerned much more with philosophical, ethical, and religious issues than with predicting technological advancements. Therefore, the London of 1984 looks remarkably similar to that of 1904. What Chesterton changes is the type of government in England, as it now chooses its king by a completely random election of a member of the populace. This is because the people of England replaced their faith in revolutions with a faith in evolution and let "natural" selection choose their leader. We are told: "Some one in the official class was made King. No one cared how: no one cared who. He was merely an universal secretary."[14] When Auberon Quin, a prankster who thinks everything is a joke, is elected as the new king, he reinstates the old custom of walling the districts of London and appointing provosts and heraldry over them as a joke. As it turns out, the provost of Notting Hill, Adam Wayne, entirely lacks a sense of humor and takes his position seriously. When the government and businessmen try to run a road through Pump Street in Notting Hill, Wayne rallies its shopkeepers and citizens to fight in battle against the opposition. They win, and keep winning, until eventually Wayne becomes the "Napoleon of Notting Hill," and a threat to everyone else. Another battle is fought in order to defeat Wayne and restore order to England. The novel ends with Quin and Wayne discovering that they are "two lobes of the same brain," one a humorist and the other

---

12. As others have noted, Chesterton ironically remained silent and unquestioning regarding the Dutch's right to be in South Africa. For example, Martin Gardner states, "He was against the war simply because he thought the Boers were right in defending their Orange Free State and their Transvaal Republic, with its rich gold mines and cheap labor. I wonder if it ever occurred to G. K. that the Dutch had as little right as the British to rule the native blacks?" ("Introduction," xvii).

13. Though Orwell's dystopia shares the same date and in fact Orwell (mostly) admired Chesterton as a writer, the similarity is probably a coincidence.

14. Chesterton, *Napoleon*, 9.

a fanatic.[15] Chesterton's larger point is that it takes both to keep sanity and order, and one without the other is dangerous.

Within his novel, Chesterton emphasizes the importance of respecting the cultural uniqueness of communities. At the beginning, a few of the main characters, namely Quin, Barker, and Lambert, meet and have lunch with the deposed President of Nicaragua. In Chesterton's future, all of the nations of the world have been swallowed up into empires and Nicaragua was the last of the small nations to go. During Quin and his friends' conversation with the ex-President of Nicaragua, the topic of cosmopolitanism arises. Barker states, "We moderns believe in a great cosmopolitan civilisation, one which shall include all the talents of all the absorbed peoples."[16] The ex-President asks Barker how he catches wild horses, to which the latter replies that he does not. Then the ex-President replies, "Precisely . . . and there ends your absorption of the talents. That is what I complain of your cosmopolitanism. When you say you want all peoples to unite, you really mean that you want all peoples to unite to learn the tricks of your people."[17] Later, this seems to be a reason for the objection to a road built through Pump Street: it will disrupt the local culture of the shops there. This situation brings to mind the objection Berry and others have had to the interstate system in the U.S., because it too has displaced local culture as it allows mass-produced and monoculture goods to travel long distances quickly and serve as a replacement. Chesterton's novel makes it clear that as long as a local culture is defending itself it is in the right, but when it enlarges its own boundaries at the expense of its neighbors, as Wayne does when he makes Notting Hill an empire, then it is in the wrong.

Interestingly, *The Flying Inn* also begins with a deposed leader. Patrick Dalroy, one of the novel's protagonists, is forced to relinquish the title "King of Ithaca" to three representatives of imperialistic world powers: Lord Ivywood, member of English Parliament; Dr. Gluck, the German Minister; and Oman Pasha, representing Turkey. Dalroy, a native Irishman, returns to his friend Mr. Pump, proprietor of the pub/inn "The Old Ship" in England. Unfortunately for them, Ivywood (under the influence of Pasha's Muslim prohibition of spirits) passes a decree outlawing the sale of alcohol

---

15. Ibid., 162.

16. Ibid., 18.

17. Ibid. The two issues of imperialism and "cultural hegemony" are closely related because they are worked out in a third issue, colonialism. When an imperial power colonizes someplace, it usually takes the best that place has to offer and in return it peddles its own economic and cultural wares, making that place more homogeneous.

anywhere lacking a proper sign, a law that prevents the poor, not the rich, from access to spirits. Therefore, Dalroy and Pump flee with sign from "The Old Ship," a keg of rum, and a wheel of cheese. They roam the English countryside, hiding from the authorities and planting the inn's sign to meet the loophole in the law and periodically justify their distribution of alcohol to the English poor, thus becoming a thorn to Ivywood. Eventually, Dalroy leads the English peasantry in an uprising against Ivywood and Pasha and wins the love of Ivywood's niece, Joan.

One way in which the differing approaches towards respecting the natural world can be seen is the ways that Dalroy and Pump treat animals compared to Ivywood and his camp. One key example concerns Ivywood's dog Quoodle, who has a whole chapter devoted to him. True to character, Ivywood regards Quoodle in very instrumental and utilitarian ways:

> Lord Ivywood did not call him Quoodle. Lord Ivywood was almost physically incapable of articulating such sounds. Lord Ivywood did not care for dogs. He cared for the Cause of Dogs, of course; and he cared still more for his own intellectual self-respect and consistency. He would never have permitted a dog in his house to be physically ill-treated; nor, for that matter, a rat; nor, for that matter, even a man. But if Quoodle was not physically ill-treated, he was at least socially neglected: and Quoodle did not like it. For dogs care for companionship more than for kindness itself.[18]

We are told that he "consulted experts" to try to sell Quoodle, but was told he was not worth much because of his mixed-breed.[19] Ivywood was also interested in his dog's ability as either a watchdog or swimming, more utilitarian reasons.[20] Chesterton has fashioned Ivywood to be his symbol of the technocrat, much like Gradgrind was for Dickens.[21] In many ways, Ivywood is a combination of MacIntyre's Rich Aesthete and Manager

---

18. Chesterton, *Flying Inn*, 498.
19. Ibid.
20. Ibid.
21. In *Orthodoxy*, Chesterton states: "But the man we see every day—the worker in Mr. Gradgrind's factory, the little clerk in Mr. Gradgrind's office—he is too mentally worried to believe in freedom. He is kept quiet with revolutionary literature. He is calmed and kept in his place by a constant succession of wild philosophies. He is a Marxian one day, a Nietzscheite the next day, a Super-man (probably) the next day; and a slave every day . . . The only man who gains by all the philosophies is Gradgrind" (159–60).

characters.[22] In contrast, Ivywood's niece "did appreciate dogs."[23] We are told "the difference remained" in Joan:

> in spite of her sophistries and ambitions; that her elemental communications were not cut, and his [Ivywood's] were. For her the sunrise was still the rising of a sun, and not the turning on of a light by a convenient cosmic servant.[24] For her the Spring was really the Season in the country, and not merely the Season in town. For her cocks and hens were natural appendages to an English house; and not (as Lord Ivywood had proved to her from an encyclopædia) animals of Indian origin, recently imported by Alexander the Great. And so for her a dog was a dog, and not one of the higher animals, nor one of the lower animals, nor something that had the sacredness of life, nor something that ought to be muzzled, nor something that ought not to be vivisected. She knew that in every practical sense proper provision would be made for the dog; as, indeed, provision was made for the yellow dogs in Constantinople by Abdul Hamid; whose life Lord Ivywood was writing for the *Progressive Potentates* series. Nor was she in the least sentimental about the dog or anxious to turn him into a pet. It simply came natural to her in passing to rub all his hair the wrong way and call him something which she instantly forgot.[25]

In Joan and Ivywood we see contrasting perspectives on Quoodle, who acts as a representative of the natural world. Whereas Ivywood and other like-minded upper class technocrats see Quoodle and others as ideas, Joan sees Quoodle as an individual whose needs need to be taken into consideration. This appreciation that Joan has for Quoodle is similar to the appreciation of particularity we discussed in chapter 2. This appreciation for particularity that Joan demonstrates can lead to a broader sentiment of appreciation for dogs in general. Lewis touched on this issue in a 1930 letter to his friend Arthur Greeves:

---

22. MacIntyre, *After Virtue*, 27–28.

23. Chesterton, *Flying Inn*, 498.

24. Cf. the opening pages of Steiner's *Real Presences*, where Steiner argues against Nietzsche's philosophy that "[w]e still speak of 'sunrise' and 'sunset'. We do so as if the Copernican model of the solar system had not replaced, ineradicably, the Ptolemaic" (3). He "wager[s]" instead that "every poet, artist, [and] composer of whom we have explicit record — predicates the presence of a realness, of a 'substantiation' . . . within language and form" (4). This seems to be Joan's (and Chesterton's) wager as well.

25. Chesterton, *Flying Inn*, 499.

> As to the business of being 'rooted' or 'at home everywhere,' I wonder are they really the opposite, or are they the same thing. I mean, don't you enjoy the Alps more precisely because you began by first learning to love in an intimate and homely way our own hills and woods? While the mere globe-trotter, starting not from a home feeling but from guide books & aesthetic chatter, feels *equally* at home everywhere only in the sense that he is really at home nowhere? It is just like the difference between vague general philanthropy . . . and learning first to love your own friends and neighbours wh. makes you *more*, not less, able to love the next stranger who comes along. If a man loveth not his brother whom he hath seen – etc. In other words, doesn't one get to the universal (either in people or in inanimate nature) *thro'* the individual – not by going off into a more generalized mash.[26]

Both Chesterton and Lewis seem to be in agreement on this principle: that our ethics and understanding of the Good, comes out of our attachment and attention to the particular goods around us. For Ivywood to have a true appreciation for canines, he first has to have an appreciation, like Joan, for Quoodle.

In this sympathetic consideration of Quoodle, a dog, is Chesterton playing the role of the ecologist? To be sure, Chesterton is not a spokesperson for ecology as we understand it by any means, but there are glimpses in his rooted ethics. This treatment of ecology is not to be expected of him at this period in history, as the term ecology and its public acknowledgement had not yet become a hypergood for society and therefore available for a complete treatment by Chesterton. Instead, Chesterton treated the environment as a part of his larger ethical framework, and thus we can see glimpses of a creational view of nature in his writings. What is missing is an explicit working out of the interaction between humans and the natural environment that shows the two coexisting without the human impulse to dominate. This public narrative had yet to emerge to the forefront, as ecology had yet to become a hypergood. When we get to Lewis, we see these human/environmental concerns starting to take shape in the public sphere, but even at that time they have yet to dominate modern ethics, as they do today for us and for Berry. With this qualification in mind, let us turn to Lewis's fiction.

Like Chesterton, Lewis saw the danger posed by the ruling class's detached instrumentalism towards individuals, communities, and the natural

---

26. Lewis, *Collected*, 912.

world as it pursued a vague concept of "progress" for humanity. MacIntyre argues:

> The problems of modern moral theory emerge clearly as the product of the failure of the Enlightenment project. On the one hand the individual free agent, freed from hierarchy and teleology, conceives of himself and is conceived of by moral philosophers as sovereign in his moral authority. On the other hand the inherited, if partially transformed rules of morality have to be found some new status, deprived as they have been of their older teleological character and their even more ancient categorical character as expressions of an ultimately divine law. If such rules cannot be found a new status which will make appeal to them rational, appeal to them will indeed appear as a mere instrument of individual desire and will. Hence there is a pressure to vindicate them either by devising some new teleology or by finding some new categorical status for them. The first project is what lends its importance to utilitarianism . . .[27]

This utilitarian outlook has its effects even in literature. Taylor acknowledges this modern phenomenon. Using "Hulme's early theory [of] poetry," he states:[28]

> In a mechanistic, utilitarian world we come to deal with things in a mechanical, conventionalized way. Our attention is turned away from things to what we are getting done through them. Ordinary prose reflects this. It deals in dead counters, which allow us to refer to things without really seeing them . . . Poetry is meant to break through this abstraction . . . The poetic image breaks away from a language of counters and gives us a fresh intuitive language which restores our vision of things.[29]

I would qualify Taylor's view by saying that prose can also be "poetic" in offering its readers a restored vision. After all, as we have seen, both Chesterton and Lewis had their imaginations baptized by George MacDonald's fiction.

As an alternative to the utilitarian vision of things, Lewis models the importance of rooted ethics in his three interplanetary novels that form a

27. MacIntyre, *After Virtue*, 62.

28. Thomas Ernest Hulme (1883–1917) was an English poet, philosopher, and critic. He associated with such poets as Ezra Pound and F. S. Flint and his ideas were influential to many modernists, notably T. S. Eliot.

29. Taylor, *Sources of the Self*, 460.

trilogy referred to today as the *Space Trilogy*. The novels were published before and during World War II in 1938, 1943, and 1945. All three novels concern a Christian philologist named Ransom. In *Out of the Silent Planet*, Ransom is kidnapped by two scientists, Devine and Weston, and taken to Malacandra (Mars) to be offered as a sacrifice to the alien beings there. In the next novel, Ransom is sent to the planet Perelandra (Venus) to prevent a Satan-possessed Weston from tricking that planet's Eve into disobeying God and turning Perelandra into a fallen planet (re-imagining the Garden of Eden story on Earth). The last novel, *That Hideous Strength*, takes place on Thulcandra (Earth) and concerns a scientific organization's plot to replace all life, except for the minds of humans, with machines and its eventual foiling by a small band of community members opposed to these goals, with Ransom as their leader. While fantastic in scope, Lewis uses these novels to pit the Christian teleology he held with the modern scientific philosophies of his time.

In *Out of the Silent Planet*, Lewis shows the modern scientific belief in progress and its instrumentalism of humanity and Nature to be egotistical, destructive, and in a word, "evil." In contrast, he presents his readers with an imaginary world in which places and their inhabitants are respected. When Weston and Devine kidnap the protagonist Ransom, their justification runs as follows: "We have learned to jump off the speck of matter on which our species began; infinity, and therefore perhaps eternity, is being put into the hands of the human race. You cannot be so small-minded as to think that the rights or the life of an individual or of a million individuals are of the slightest importance in comparison with this."[30] Of course Ransom disagrees, stating, "I consider your philosophy of life raving lunacy. I suppose all that stuff about infinity and eternity means that you think you are justified in doing anything . . . on the off chance that some creatures or other descendants from man as we know him may crawl about a few centuries longer in some part of the universe."[31] Weston replies, "Yes—anything whatever . . . and all educated opinion—for I do not call classics and history and such trash education—is entirely on my side."[32] Here Lewis raises a crucial argument for the importance of the humanities in education, which is a significant part of my own argument. The humanities—and art includ-

---

30. Lewis, *Out*, 29. Two decades later, Lewis's fiction becomes a reality. See chapter 1, n. 13.

31. Ibid., 29–30.

32. Ibid., 30.

ing literature in particular—are an essential part of human culture that help us stay ethically fixed within a larger tradition. These limits prevent us from transgressing the boundaries of our place and therefore disrespecting the individuals, communities, and natural world around us.[33]

Lewis shows how these ethical boundaries help communities coexist through mutual respect in his depiction of the inhabitants of Malacandra, who consist of three species akin to humans in essence, though not in form. The community life of these three species, who have learned to live successfully (through culture and tradition) in their place and in harmony with each other and their environments, acts as a foil for the imperialistic, Wellsian motives of Weston and Devine, as well as for the non-harmonious ways in which humans live on Thulcandra. After all, in 1938 the nation states in Europe were about to confront the very real consequences of overstepped boundaries that led to World War II. On Malacandra the three species (or metaphorical nation states) were the sorns, hrossa, and pfifltriggi. Though not intermixing, these three species respected each other and realized the unique and important roles they served to the whole planet (ecosystem).[34] This can be clearly seen in a discovery Ransom makes while staying with the sorn, who are the most philosophical of the species. He stumbles upon a "monolithic avenue" of stones containing carved depictions of the history of Malacandra.[35] The history contains not only depictions of activities performed by each of the three human-like species, but also depictions of other animal life and of the history of the solar system as well. Lewis is showing the importance of the humanities—specifically history and philosophy—in preserving a story that assigns the various parts of creation places in an order, thus providing them with limits to respect. Like the sorn, the hrossa also preserve history and tradition, but their chosen medium is

33. A recent book (2011) that purportedly asserts the ethical importance of the humanities, while also rejecting the belief in a shared ethical standard, is *All Things Shining* by Hubert Dreyfus and Sean Dorrance Kelly. For a brief overview of their argument, see this *New York Times* Sunday Book Review: http://www.nytimes.com/2011/01/23/books/review/Neiman-t.html. See also this lively exchange between the authors and Gary Wills: http://www.nybooks.com/articles/archives/2011/may/26/all-things-shining-exchange/.

34. So, is Lewis suggesting segregation or separation of species as the way to insure harmony? From Lewis's strong comments about the dangers of modern "ethics" in the *Abolition of Man*, quoted below, I believe he would have opposed forced segregation. His point in *Out of the Silent Planet* is that culturally different communities could respect each other's differences and live in harmony, as long as they derived their ethical philosophy from the same external source, which he called the *Tao* in the *Abolition of Man*.

35. Lewis, *Out*, 110–11.

poetry. These cultural artifacts have allowed Malacandra, an old planet, to exist in an "unfallen" state compared to Thulcandra (Earth).

To underscore the importance given even to non-human life on Malacandra, Lewis provides an interesting exchange between Ransom and Hyoi, a hross. On Malacandra there exists a shark-like animal called a hnakra that is carnivorous and antagonistic towards the hrossa and therefore the hrossa must occasionally hunt and kill. In trying to understand the nature of "bentness" (sin) on Malacandra, Ransom questions Hyoi about the hnakra. Hyoi replies:

> Oh, but that is so different. I long to kill this *hnakra* as he also longs to kill me. I hope that my ship will be the first and I first in my ship with my straight spear when the black jaws snap. And if he kills me, my people will mourn and my brothers will desire still more to kill him. But they will not wish that there were no *hnéraki*; nor do I. How can I make you understand, when you do not understand the poets? The *hnakra* is our enemy, but he is also our beloved.[36]

Here, Lewis's views seem similar to a Native American perspective towards nature, that it is to be loved and respected for what it is, even if that means it is antagonistic towards us. This way of looking at the world is a very difficult and foreign concept, especially to a culture that is obsessed with things like bug spray and sanitary wipes, scientific products designed to exterminate unwanted parts of nature. Of course, this does not entirely work as planned and resistant bugs, bacteria, and virus strains develop, but that does not change our instrumentalist perspective towards the environment. Lewis depicts a nightmarish form of this mentality in *That Hideous Strength,* when he makes removing all non-desirable vegetation from the Earth one of the goals of the scientific technocrat agency N.I.C.E. After Mr. Winter admits his "fond[ness] of trees," Filostrato replies:

> Oh, yes . . . The pretty trees, the garden trees. But not the savages. I put the rose in my garden, but not the brier. The forest tree is a weed. But I tell you I have seen the civilized tree in Persia. It was a French *attaché* who had it because he was in a place where trees did not grow. It was made of metal. A poor, crude thing. But how if it were perfected? Light, made of aluminium. So natural, it would even deceive."

"It would hardly be the same as a real tree," said Winter.

---

36. Ibid., 76.

"But consider the advantages! . . . At present, I allow, we must have forests, for the atmosphere. Presently we find a chemical substitute. And then, why any natural trees? I foresee nothing but the *art* tree all over the earth. In fact, we *clean* the planet."[37]

Eventually, Filostrato's train of thought leads him to reject birds, all organic life, even dirt and the bodies of humans. What Lewis argues here, as he did in *The Abolition of Man*, is the danger of an unrooted morality that has no way to check the type of scientific progress that would damn the physical in pursuit of the eternal spiritual. This is similar to the pursuit of heaven by many modern Christians at the expense of the environment, as lamented by Berry and others.

In fact, Jason Peters has recently discussed Berry's orthodox rejection of this heresy in his essay "Education, Heresy, and the 'Deadly Disease of the World.'" Examining Berry's companion essays "Why I Am Not Going to Buy a Computer" and "Feminism, the Body, and the Machine," Peters argues that the dualism between body and spirit that Berry rejects is the heresy of Gnosticism that permeates our culture. Quoting Berry, Peters comments:

> "The danger most immediately to be feared in 'technological progress,'" Berry says, "is the degradation and obsolescence of the body"—that's Gnosticism. "Implicit in the technological revolution from the beginning has been a new version of an old dualism"—that's Gnosticism in its specifically Manichaean iteration—"one always destructive, and now more destructive than ever." The education of which Berry long ago declared himself skeptical perpetuates both heresies, and the result is absurdity and perversion—a perversion that has now become the deadly disease of the world.[38]

How did Berry acquire this orthodoxy? Peters states, "Berry came to this orthodoxy not by studying but by meditating poetry and place, by attending to soil and practicing the disciplines by which it is maintained . . . A great many of us, by contrast, abstracted from the soil and disinclined toward the domestic arts, languish under a resuscitated gnosticism that our education perpetuates."[39] Peters argues that Berry rejects the "bestialism

---

37. Lewis, *That*, 169.
38. Peters, "Education," 274.
39. Ibid., 273.

and angelism that follow upon our flight from the flesh."[40] For Chesterton, Lewis, and Berry an ethics rooted in a particular place allows one to resist and reject the Gnostic heresy. Likewise, when the humanities encourage active involvement with physical people, places, and things it bridges this schism between the life of the mind and the body.

In addition to the *Space Trilogy*, Lewis emphasizes rooted ethics in his *Narnia* series. Perhaps one of the clearest examples of the difference between those with and without rooted ethics occurs in book six of the *Chronicles of Narnia* series.[41] In *The Magician's Nephew*, Lewis provides a stark contrast between two types: a magician/scientist type and an agrarian/steward/king type. The novel concerns the creation of Narnia by Aslan the Lion, who represents Christ in Lewis's imaginative world. Through trickery, Uncle Andrew, a magician/scientist sends his nephew Digory and Digory's friend Polly to a "World between the Worlds" consisting of several pools of water. Each pool of water leads to its own separate world. Digory and Polly end up in a dead world and awaken a witch who has been under a spell. This witch, Jadis, forces the children to take her back to London so she can rule our world. The children lead Jadis, Uncle Andrew, a cabby and his horse back to the World Between the Woods and eventually to Narnia, where they witness its creation. Aslan appoints the cabby and his wife to be king and queen of Narnia, banishes the Witch, and sends the children and Uncle Andrew back home.

Lewis characterizes the magician/scientist type in two primary ways. First, they are utilitarian, which leads them to be cruel to people, animals, and the environment. For example, Lewis makes a point to stress Uncle Andrew's cruelty towards guinea-pigs in his experiments.[42] He states, "My

---

40. Ibid., 274. Perhaps one of the strongest Gnostic voices in our time is that of Harold Bloom. In a recent article critical of this aspect of Bloom, R. V. Young states: "While he [Bloom] gazes unblinkingly at the devastation wrought upon the tradition by the postmodern assault, he is blind to the intimate and indispensable bond between the secular 'canon' and the Faith informing its necessary model, the scriptural canon. Western civilization is the cultural embodiment of Christendom; when its cultural heart stops beating, all that is left is a corpse" (19–20). Young's commentary runs parallel to Taylor's, as both recognize the inseparable bond between the Judeo-Christian tradition and the Western culture of which we are heirs.

41. Though the action of the novel precedes the others and is thus labeled as book one in contemporary reprints, Lewis chronologically wrote the book sixth, in 1955.

42. Unlike PETA's exaggerated position that sees humans as a sub-species of animals and often gives more rights to other animals than humans, Lewis is consistent in his position that humans are distinct from animals and are privileged in the Creational Order.

earlier experiments were all failures. I tried them on guinea-pigs. Some of them only died. Some exploded like little bombs—."[43] Digory, who we are told "once had a guinea-pig of his own," calls these actions "a jolly cruel thing to do," and receives this reply from his Uncle: "That's what the creatures were there for. I'd bought them myself."[44] Later, when Digory asks his uncle why he sends guinea-pigs, Polly, and Digory into the other world as a part of his experiment instead of going himself, Uncle Andrew exclaims:

> Me? Me? . . . The boy must be mad! A man at my time of life, and in my state of health, to risk the shock and the dangers of being flung suddenly into a different universe?
>
> You don't understand. I am the great scholar, the magician, the adept who is *doing* the experiment. Of course I need subjects to do the experiment *on*. Bless my soul, you'll be telling me next that I ought to have asked the guinea-pigs permission before I used *them*![45]

In *The Magician's Nephew* we see these contrasting views towards guinea-pigs as creatures. For Uncle Andrew, buying them constitutes owning them and therefore gives him the right to treat them any way he pleases in service of some "higher good," which we really see in the novel amounts to glory-seeking. For Digory, the animals were to be treated fairly and cared for. Of course, Lewis here seems to condone pet ownership and thus asserts that humans can exercise some will over animals, as long as the animals are cared for. Lewis strongly opposed vivisection. In his essay, "Vivisection," he claims that the only true argument in favor of it comes from a Christian perspective that believes humans and animals are distinct creatures, though he believes this should compel us to "prove ourselves better than the beasts precisely by the fact of acknowledging duties to them which they do not acknowledge to us."[46] The real danger, however, lies elsewhere for Lewis. He states:

> But of course the vast majority of vivisectors have no such theological background. They are most of them naturalistic and

---

However, he clearly has problems with an abuse of that privilege in the treatment of animals, devoting a chapter in *The Problem of Pain* to "Animal Pain," as well as the essays "Vivisection" and "The Pains of Animals: A Problem in Theology" to the subject.

43. Lewis, *Magician's*, 21.
44. Ibid.
45. Ibid., 22–23.
46. Lewis, "Vivisection," 452.

Darwinian . . . The very same people who will most contemptuously brush aside any consideration of animal suffering if it stands in the way of 'research' will also, on the another context, most vehemently deny that there is any radical difference between man and the other animals . . . If loyalty to our own species, preference for man simply because we are men, is not a sentiment, then what is? . . .

But the most sinister thing about modern vivisection is this. If a mere sentiment justifies cruelty, why stop at a sentiment for the whole human race? There is also a sentiment for the white man against the black, for a *Herrenvolk* against the non-Aryans, for 'civilized' or 'progressive' peoples against 'savage' or 'backward' peoples . . . Once the old Christian idea of a total difference in kind between man and beast has been abandoned, then no argument for experiments on animals can be found which is not also an argument for experiments on inferior men.[47]

Certainly we see this slippery sentiment exhibited in Uncle Andrew. He tells Digory, "Men like me who possess hidden wisdom, are freed from common rules just as we are cut off from common pleasures. Ours, my boy, is a high and lonely destiny."[48] Here we see Uncle Andrew claiming for himself special status above other humans, therefore justifying his abuses of them, but his reasoning is based upon his own sentiment. Later, Queen Jadis tells the children something similar, except she represents what Uncle Andrew will become if he continues down his slippery slope of sentiment. After telling the children about a war with her sister that destroyed both their kingdoms, Polly questions her about "[a]ll the ordinary people . . . who'd never done you any harm . . . [including] the women, and the children, and the animals."[49] Jadis replies, "I was the Queen. They were all *my* people. What else were they there for but to do my will."[50] She continues, "You must learn, child, that what would be wrong for you or for any of the common people is not wrong in a great Queen such as I. The weight of the world is on our shoulders. We must be freed from all rules. Ours is a high and lonely destiny."[51] Digory (and Lewis's readers) immediately recognize the parallel in Andrew and Jadis's words, confirming that they represent

47. Ibid., 452–53.
48. Lewis, *Magician's*, 18.
49. Ibid., 61.
50. Ibid.
51. Ibid., 62.

the same dangerous mentality that views individuals and the natural world instrumentally.[52]

Second, magician/scientists are imperial and colonial; they dominate and use up people and resources in one place and then move on to the next to do the same. Certainly, this is clear in Queen Jadis's actions. Having used up her own world warring with her sister, she sees the children's breaking of her spell as an opportunity for her to dominate another world and use it up. She only views others as being instrumentally in service to her; for her, their purpose is not to seek goods on their own but to serve her and her ideology. Likewise, when Uncle Andrew sees the creation of Narnia, he only sees in it the instrumental potential to serve him. Upon seeing all of the newly created animals, he thinks, "If I were a younger man, now—perhaps I could get some lively young fellow to come here first. One of those big game hunters. Something might be made of this country."[53] Later he thinks, "I have discovered a world where everything is bursting with life and growth . . . The commercial possibilities of this country are unbounded."[54] The final stage in this instrumental perspective involves the desire to extend life as long as possible: "And then as regards oneself . . . There's no knowing how long I might live if I settled here."[55] Jadis and Andrew both see Narnia as a resource to be used up in service of themselves, not as a good Creation to be respected.

In contrast, Lewis provides the model of the agrarian/steward/king type. Unlike the magician/scientist, this type submits to authority—sees the hierarchy of which it is a part—and respects limits. This leads to the other primary characteristic of this type: respect for other people, communities, and the natural world. One way this respect is exhibited is in a willingness to be attentive to the world around, to listen, rather than act upon. Unlike Uncle Andrew and Jadis, who refuse to stop acting as they move (and seek to conquer) from place to place, the Cabby "struck up at once a harvest thanksgiving hymn, all about crops being 'safely gathered in'" when he witnesses Narnia's creation. When the others start to argue with each other,

---

52. Today's politicians imply such views, for example, when the label "terrorist" makes humans fair game for "above the law" practices such as Predator drone strikes, perpetual detainment without trial, or interrogation methods that include torture.

53. Ibid., 109.

54. Ibid., 111.

55. Ibid., 112.

he states, "'Old your noise, everyone . . . I want to listen to the moosic."⁵⁶ Later he asserts, "Watchin' and listenin' 's the thing at present; not talking."⁵⁷ Lewis is demonstrating the Cabby's participation in the good life as he is attentive to the external Good that he sees. This type of activity is one that Uncle Andrew and Jadis cannot comprehend—they see the creation of Narnia either as a threat to their safety or as resource to be exploited.

To be fair, Lewis was not an ecologist, like Berry. He, like Chesterton, was writing before the term "ecology" had even been coined. Nevertheless, Matthew Dickerson and David O'Hara see in Lewis an "integrated worldview," claiming "his Christian story is one that calls the world good and hospitable and that calls for reverential and humble response on the part of humans. His is a voice that gives the lie to the 'Abrahamic' narrative of domination." ⁵⁸ Of course, his views will not seem developed or consistent enough to some modern ecologists. For example, Margarita Carretero-González praises his acknowledgement of the importance of non-human life, but also points out how he still operates out of an anthropocentric worldview, making him problematic for many environmentalists today. She believes "the issue at stake here" is that "Lewis had complete faith in the dogma that humans had been appointed by God to be the center of the universe and this assertion can hardly be reconciled with deep ecological ethics."⁵⁹ Nevertheless, Carretero-González states, "In focusing too much on the negative aspects of the Narnian world, we may lose the benefit of seeing the environmental perspective Lewis does entertain, and there is certainly much in this regard . . . to celebrate and enjoy."⁶⁰

In Berry, we of course find the most fleshed-out Judeo-Christian ecological philosophy, rooted in an attentive respect for the natural world, rather than an instrumental condescension. Like Chesterton, Berry is concerned for the way autocrats like Ivywood take an instrumentalist stance towards individuals in other communities, even if it is for their own "good." Writing of the "tyranny of charity," Berry states: "An agency or bureau or institution cannot exercise taste and judgment, cannot be motivated by love or compassion, cannot value a man for his industry or his art or his pride; they are abstractions themselves and must deal with people as

---

56. Ibid., 103.
57. Ibid., 106.
58. Dickerson and O'Hara, *Narnia*, 258
59. Carretero-González, "Sons of Adam," 96.
60. Ibid., 109.

abstractions."[61] He continues, "To give a man bread when he needs a tool is as inept and unfeeling as to give him a stone when he needs bread, and this painful clumsiness is inherent in the generalizations of the social planners and the organized charities. Their most 'humane' endeavors almost necessarily involve an attitude toward humanity that debases it."[62]

One way Berry sees individuals as sacred can be seen in his use of the terms "respect" and "affection." As we have already seen, Berry's philosophical vision is often filtered through an economic lens. He thus contrasts how an authentic economy should treat individuals with how our industrial economy currently treats them. He says, "The right economy is right insofar as it respects the source, respects the power of the source to resurge, and does not ask too much."[63] He gives topsoil as an example of how individual things have value beyond what the industrial economy places on them: "[Topsoil's] value is inestimable; we must value it, beyond whatever price we put on it, by *respecting* it."[64] In contrast, "The industrial economy . . . reduces the value of a thing to its market price, and it sets the market price in accordance with the capacity of a thing to be made into another kind of thing."[65] Elsewhere, Berry asserts that "people, places, and things cannot be well used without affection. To be well used, creatures and places must be used sympathetically, just as they must be known sympathetically to be well known."[66] For examples, he states:

> The economist to whom it is of no concern whether or not a family loves its farm will almost inevitably aid and abet the destruction of family farming. The "animal scientist" to whom it is of no concern whether animals will suffer will almost inevitably aid and abet the destruction of the decent old ideal of animal husbandry and, as a consequence, increase the suffering of animals. I hope that my

---

61. Berry, *Long-Legged*, 9. For some, Berry may sound here like a libertarian. However, I believe Berry makes it clear in his essays that there is a role government should play in creating and enforcing laws that foster greater local community well-being. What he is critical of are policies that are impersonal; charity should be motivated out of a personal relationship between neighbors, because of the respect involved. Love, the greatest expression of respect, can only truly exist if people are known personally, not as statistics.

62. Ibid., 9–10.

63. Berry, "Nation," 72.

64. Ibid., 73.

65. Ibid., 73.

66. Berry, "Argument," 82.

country may be delivered from the remote, cold abstractions of university science.[67]

Lest we think Berry only has qualms with university science, he has this to say about the humanities: "The humanities have been destructive not because they have been misapplied, but because they have been so frequently understood by their academic stewards as not applicable."[68] For example, he states, "A poem . . . is a relic as soon as it is composed; it can be taught, but it cannot teach . . . I hope that my country may be delivered from the objectivity of the humanities."[69] As we saw earlier in our discussion of Lewis's *Space Trilogy*, the humanities should be doing the crucial task of placing students within a larger tradition, and this task cannot be accomplished if poems, novels, and plays are taught as artifacts divorced from their frameworks.

A good example of how Berry values humans as individuals whose pursuit of the good life must be respected can be seen in his criticism of our modern culture's "attitude toward work."[70] He is sharply critical of how modern culture has shied away from "the manual work necessary to the long-term preservation of the land," instead opting for a "rush toward mechanization, automation, and computerization."[71] As a consequence, agribusiness has eliminated the need for humans to do what Berry sees as good work in the country, and thus our cities have become overcrowded with the "permanently unemployable."[72] He asks, "One wonders what the authors of our Constitution would have thought of that category, 'permanently unemployable.'"[73] This leads Berry to ask further questions about the *telos* of humans: "The great question that hovers over this issue, one that we have dealt with mainly by indifference, is the question of what people are *for*. Is their greatest dignity in unemployment? Is the obsolescence of human beings now our social goal?"[74] Berry believes that work is essential for the well being of humans. This mandate for work can be traced back

67. Ibid.
68. Ibid.
69. Ibid., 83.
70. Berry, "What," 107. See Taylor, *Sources of the Self*, "God Loveth Adverbs" for a discussion of the Protestant work ethic inherited by moderns (211–33).
71. Ibid.
72. Ibid., 106.
73. Ibid.
74. Ibid., 107.

to Genesis, when God has Adam name the animals and gives him and his descendants the task of "subdue[ing]" the earth.[75] In the second version of the Creation story, we are given a less controversial description: "The Lord God took the man and put him in the garden of Eden to work it and keep it."[76] In her poem "Tragic Error," Denise Levertov looks at our misreading of the mandate to "subdue" in Genesis, expressing well this original understanding of work: "Surely we were to have been | earth's mind, mirror, reflective source. | Surely our task | was to have been | to love the earth, | to dress and keep it like Eden's garden."[77] So from the very beginning, pre-Fall, work (at least agricultural or cultivating work) was an essential part of what constituted humanness and was deemed "good." Therefore, Berry rightfully takes issue with industrialism's purpose (or at least, byproduct) of taking away work from humans. Taking away work leads to an abstraction of humans into a category, the "permanently unemployable," and this opens the door to greater abstractions, like an absentee economy.

Berry has a lot to say about the lack of respect an absentee economy shows in its abstraction of people, communities, and the natural world. He states:

> Living as we now do in almost complete dependence on a global economy, we are put inevitably into a position of ignorance and irresponsibility ... We can connect ourselves to the globe as a whole only by means of a global economy that, without knowing the earth, plunders it for us ... To build houses here, we clear-cut the forests there. To have air-conditioning here, we strip-mine mountains there. To drive our cars here, we sink our oil wells there. It is an absentee economy. Most people aren't using or destroying what they can see.[78]

Of this type of economy Patrick Deneen states, "Modern economic systems tend toward abstraction, replacing exchange that closely demonstrates the connections between work and its products with complex financial and

---

75. Gen 1:28. This term, of course, has been the subject of much debate and derision. Starting with Lynn White Jr.'s "The Historical Roots of Our Ecological Crisis" in 1967, many have blamed the Judeo-Christian tradition's misreading of Genesis 1 as a mandate for humans to use up the Earth. Of course, many others have rebutted this contention and have sought to return to a pre-Enlightenment understanding of Genesis. See Steven Bouma-Prediger, *For the Beauty of the Earth*.

76. Gen 2:15.

77. Levertov, "Tragic Error," 69, lines 10–15.

78. Berry, "Conservation," 37.

monetary interactions that obscure those relations."[79] This type of economy exists because technocrats make decisions based upon ideas and not real people and communities. Berry states, "The present practice of handing down from on high policies and technologies developed without consideration of the nature and needs of the land and the people has not worked, and it cannot work."[80]

Berry calls this type of economic practice "colonization." He states, "The economic principle is everywhere the same: a domestic colonialism that extracts an immense wealth from our rural landscapes, returning as near nothing as possible or nothing or worse than nothing to the land and the people."[81] Elsewhere he says, "[T]hinking to transcend our definition as fallen creatures, we have only colonized more and more territory eastward of Eden."[82] Furthermore, says Berry, "The global 'free market' is free to the corporations precisely because it dissolves the boundaries of the old national colonialisms, and replaces them with a new colonialism without restraints or boundaries."[83] Berry terms this abstract economic practice "the colonization of the future," saying, "What has drawn the Modern World into being is a strange, almost occult yearning for the future."[84] Not surprisingly, he begins this chapter in *The Unsettling of America* (from which the previous quote was derived) with a quote from *That Hideous Strength*, which runs thus: "Dreams of the far future destiny of man were dragging up from its shallow and unquiet grave the old dream of Man as God. The very experience of the dissecting room and the pathological laboratory were breeding a conviction that the stifling of all deep-set repugnances was the first essential for progress."[85] Once again, the yearning for the future

79. Deneen, "Wendell Berry," 308.
80. Berry, "Argument," 81.
81. Berry, "Simple," 59.
82. Berry, "Two Economies," 128.

83. Berry, "Total Economy," 182. Thomas Friedman's recent *New York Times* essay "Made in the World" succinctly discusses this issue. Friedman states, "There is a big gap in how C.E.O.'s and political leaders look at the world." He argues that while politicians have an obligation to the citizens of their nations, multi-national corporations are constrained by no such boundaries; they make their goods overseas to minimize costs and sell to a global, not national, market. Friedman states, "Therein lies the tension. So many of 'our' companies actually see themselves now as citizens of the world. But Obama is president of the United States." Berry would probably add that many, if not most, of these companies are not behaving as ideal "citizens," interested in the public good.

84. Berry, *Unsettling*, 56.
85. Ibid., 50.

demonstrated in this passage exemplifies what Arendt sees in humanity's flight from earth. Philosophically and theologically, then, Berry and Lewis see at the back of the worldview of abstracting others to instrumentally achieve "progress" the old desire to escape our human condition and become like God. What is really at issue here, therefore, is our rootlessness within the larger creational order that dictates how we are to live towards the other things within that order.

In contrast to the absentee economy, Berry espouses what we have already seen he calls the Great Economy.[86] According to Berry, the Great Economy "seek[s] the Kingdom of God *first*; that is, it gives an obviously necessary priority to the Great Economy over any little economy made within it. The passage [Matt. 6] also clearly includes nature within the Great Economy, and it affirms the goodness, indeed the sanctity, of natural creatures."[87] Berry asserts that humans must make their own little economies in order to live in this world, but they should be subservient to the Great Economy. The problem he sees with the industrial economy is that it "does not see itself as a little economy; it sees itself as the only economy . . . The industrial economy is based on invasion and pillage of the Great Economy."[88] He states, "Sometime between, say, Pope's verses on the Chain of Being in *An Essay on Man* and Blake's "London," the dominant minds had begun to see the human race, not as a part or a member of Creation, but outside and opposed to it."[89] However, he asserts, "There is no 'outside' to the Great Economy, no escape into either specialization or generality, no 'time off . . .'." Our modern perspective of viewing ourselves as separate from Creation is one of the frameworks that Taylor calls "unquestioned fact."[90] It is also one of the most pervasive (and destructive). We can presume that we are outside the membership that includes us, but that presumption only damages the membership—and ourselves, of course, along with it."[91] Our choices as earth dwellers will therefore have an impact on our environment and thus must be considered (farming practices, for example). Berry does

---

86. In a move similar to Lewis's using the *Tao* as his "neutral" term for shared ethics, Berry uses the Great Economy as his "neutral" term for the Kingdom of God.

87. Berry, "Two Economies," 119.

88. Ibid., 126.

89. Ibid., 131.

90. Taylor, *Sources of the Self*, 17.

91. Berry, "Two Economies," 136.

not deny this reality, nor does he expect little economies/communities to be completely self-sufficient:

> Of course, everything needed locally cannot be produced locally. But a viable neighborhood is a community, and a viable community is made up of neighbors who cherish and protect what they have in common. This is the principle of subsistence. A viable community, like a viable farm, protects its own production capacities. It does not import products that it can produce for itself. And it does not export local products until local needs have been met.[92]

We saw earlier in chapter 2 models for both types of little economies. The type of little economy that tries to live outside of the Great Economy, exemplified by Troy's farm and Meickelberger's agribusiness, buys out its neighbors and seeks to increase its production by importing borrowed wealth and ignoring limits of every kind. This type of economy led to the reduction in health of its adherents (seen in Meikelberger's ulcer) and in the surrounding community (loss of neighbors). In contrast, the Amish farmer Troyer ran his little economy with respect for the Great Economy and by accepting the limits that economy imposed on him had both a flourishing farm and community.

In fact, it is at the end of the novel *Remembering* that Berry emphasizes the *telos* of restoration in the Judeo-Christian tradition. Andy, we may recall, has returned home from San Francisco, where he had contemplated abandoning his family and past. When he arrives home he is exhausted and he falls asleep under an oak tree on his farm. He has a vision of a "dark man" leading him further and further into the future and up a hill on his property, where he eventually gets a glimpse of Port William. This is what he sees:

> The dark man points ahead of them; Andy looks and sees the town and the fields around it, Port William and its countryside as he never saw or dreamed them, the signs everywhere upon them of the care of a longer love than any who have lived there have ever imagined. The houses are clean and white, and great trees stand among them and spread over them. The fields lie around the town, divided by rows of such trees as stand in the town and in the woods, each field more beautiful than all the rest. Over town and fields the one great song sings, and is answered everywhere; every leaf and flower and grass blade sings. And in the fields and

---

92. Berry, "Total Economy," 192.

the town, walking, standing, or sitting under the trees, resting and talking together in the peace of a sabbath profound and bright, are people of such beauty that he weeps to see them. He sees that these are the membership of one another and of the place and of the song or light in which they live and move.[93]

The people "appear as children corrected and clarified."[94] They, like their communities and the natural world, have been restored. Berry's message is clear: people, communities, and the natural world are not resources to be used up or collateral damage to changing philosophical fads, but they are eternal, good, and will someday be restored.

This awareness should translate into a rooted ethical perspective that respects the Judeo-Christian "present, not yet" nature of individuals, communities, and nature.[95] Respecting all things means acknowledging their place in a larger hierarchical framework and accepting the limits that are implicit to this framework. Accepting these limits will prevent the destruction caused by imperialism and colonialism, because those institutions are built upon a rejection of limits, easily seen in the obvious greed that accompanies them. This rooted ethical perspective may sound idealistic, but for Chesterton, Lewis, Berry, and many others, it is the starting place to fix the problems we face in our confused, modern society.

---

93. Berry, *Remembering*, 221.

94. Ibid.

95. For Jews, while God has a very real influence on earth during the Diaspora, the Messiah has not yet come to restore order. For Christians, Christ started that restoration while on earth, but it will not be complete until the Second Coming.

4

WHOLENESS, THE HUMANITIES, AND PLACE

Thus far we have examined many similarities in the writings of Chesterton, Lewis, and Berry. We have explored their decisions to return to and set down roots in a tradition, rather than listen to the exploratory narratives of many of their modern contemporaries. Besides this mutual return, we have seen how their ethical and economic philosophies have grown up from these roots. In this chapter, we will take up in a new and fuller way, based upon what we have learned, the question posed in the introduction and analyze what these authors have to say to the question, "What does it mean to be human?" We will also see how these authors and their work give new meaning and significance, especially regarding the importance of wholeness, to the place of the humanities in a liberal arts education.

To begin, let us borrow and appropriate a definition from J. Scott Bryson to help us define the aspects of modern culture that are among the most problematic for our authors. In his recent book *The West Side of Any Mountain*, Bryson identifies three characteristics that are needed to confront the "distinctly contemporary problems and issues" of modern culture: "[A]n ecological and biocentric perspective recognizing the interdependent nature of the world; a deep humility with regard to our relationships with human and nonhuman nature; and an intense skepticism that usually leads to condemnation of an overtechnologized modern world and a warning concerning the very real potential for ecological catastrophe."[1]

---

1. Bryson, *West Side*, 2.

The problematic aspects of modernity Bryson implies are as follows: a non-ecological and egocentric perspective that, to borrow Taylor's term, disengages humans from nature and other humans;[2] a deep arrogance with regard to our relationships with human and nonhuman nature; and an exclusive reliance on disengagement and its correlative "objectification,"[3] a reliance that usually fosters an unquestioned overuse of technology, regardless of the consequences of its use. These three characteristics underscore a larger issue: a loss of communal identity that is a mark of modern culture and has been a point of contention among philosophers, theologians, historians, and sociologists for over a century.

As we have seen, thinkers such as Arendt, MacIntyre, and Taylor have traced the historical origins of our modern crisis of human identity. Their work is crucial in showing how our modern ideas about humanness and our planetary place have deemphasized Aristotle's important link between place and ethics, and also in showing how many of our modern beliefs have their roots in a secularizing of the Judeo-Christian tradition. This deemphasis has helped create much of the identity turmoil felt today. In *After Virtue*, MacIntyre claims "it is worth remembering Aristotle's insistence that the virtues find their place not just in the life of the individual, but in the life of the city"—or today, a community whose members share a similar faith and tradition—"and that the individual is indeed intelligible only as a *politikon zôon*."[4] In *Sources of the Self*, Taylor shows how the Aristotelian and Catholic dichotomy that elevated contemplation of the good over the labor of everyday life was rejected and overturned by the Reformation.[5] When the reformers rejected the institutionalized church, they placed the saving relationship between God and his church in individuals.[6] This change emphasized an individual's place in the world, rather than emphasizing the importance of a community of shared values.

While it is true that many Christians over the centuries have sought to create a world culture, the same can be said for many other institutions—religious, political, economical, and cultural. The problem is not with the orthodox root of Christianity, which is a relational state of being concerning human beings' relationship with God and with Creation, including

2. Taylor, *Sources of the Self*, 160.
3. Ibid.
4. MacIntyre, *After Virtue*, 150.
5. Taylor, *Sources of the Self*, 211–12.
6. Ibid., 216–17.

other humans. In fact, in Acts 2 we find that the first Christians did live together in small communities—it was not until later that, first, the church became more and more institutionalized and, second, the Reformation led to an emphasis on the individual. Thus, the concept of a world community made up of individuals can be seen as an issue for Christianity as it became increasingly assimilated with the changing culture around it. Not all authors, particularly Christians, have succumbed to one or the other of these issues and so what is needed is an examination of those Christian authors centered on the question, "How can the literature of Christian authors show us how to return to a *relational* emphasis on place, local communities, and ethics?" One possible answer, of course, is that this literature is grounded in hypergoods that promote just such a relational emphasis.

When we consider these hypergoods that emphasize relationships, Berry is of course the most overt, due to a more narrow focus on this issue in his essays, and his having located his fiction almost exclusively in the same community of Port William. But we get to Berry through Chesterton and Lewis. As we have seen, all three authors explore humanity's relation to places, ethics, and things. By things, I include nature, humans, and man-made objects. However, each author in a foundational work offers his own unique perspective on the three categories. As Chesterton shows in *Orthodoxy*, it is orthodoxy that gives humans the appropriate relationships to places, ethics, and things. Lewis, in *The Abolition of Man*, insisted that only an acceptance of the *Tao*, or absolute Truth (a set of common objective values held across cultures and eras), could properly cultivate right relationships to these categories. For Berry, health (defined as wholeness) is the primary measure for humans and places. Though he discusses this perspective throughout much of his work, perhaps an early and key instance can be seen in his book *The Unsettling of America*, particularly in the chapter titled "The Body and the Earth." Let's briefly examine a few passages in each of these three works, beginning with Chesterton, to construct a framework for the values/virtues infused throughout their literature.

In *Orthodoxy*, Chesterton argues from his own personal experiences. He shows how his discovery of orthodox Judeo-Christian values helped him make sense of his life and its relationship to the universe. As he says, "The spike of dogma fitted exactly into the hole in the world—it had evidently been meant to go there—and then the strange thing began to happen. When once these two parts of the two machines had come together, one after another, all the other parts fitted and fell in with an eerie exactitude."[7] Therefore, orthodoxy allows Chesterton to make sense of the relationships between places, ethics, and things. For example, because Nature was created as good, it is to be respected, but not objectified as a commodity. Likewise, humans are also created as good and to be respected, but not made exclusive ends. These principles of orthodoxy put in proper relation ethics between humans and places.

Lewis, in *The Abolition of Man*, argues from a more philosophical approach.[8] In part three, he describes the consequences of rejecting a common ethic, or *Tao*, for humanity and Nature. He states, "In the older systems both the kind of man the teachers wished to produce and their motives for producing him were prescribed by the *Tao*—a norm to which the teachers themselves were subject and from which they claimed no liberty to depart."[9] In other words, there was a transcendent order of common values that guided all members of the community, from the top of the power structure to the bottom. He then argues that by rejecting this common system of values, humans lose what separates them from Nature, and thus are left to be guided by the same impulses that guide Nature. As he states, "Man's final conquest has proved to be the abolition of Man."[10] Rejecting these common values, therefore, has dramatic consequences for places, ethics, and things. The only guiding "ethic" left is that of Nature, whose first instinct is self-preservation and self-assertion. Of course, there are many instances when self-preservation or self-assertion can be proper goals, such as our natural inclinations to nourish ourselves or to escape danger. However, if our only guiding ethic was this instinct, we would be in conflict with regards to such ethics as bravery, because we must be willing to accept, rather than flee from danger, in order to achieve some other purpose, whether to save another's life or to save our own. Regarding this instinct of self-preservation and self-assertion, Lewis states, "When all that says 'it is good' has been debunked, what says 'I want' remains."[11] Similarly, he states, "If you will not obey the *Tao*, or else commit suicide, obedience to impulse (and therefore, in the long run, to mere 'nature') is the only course left open."[12] What is

---

7. Chesterton, *Orthodoxy*, 114.

8. Though written in a WWII context, Lewis's basic argument applies to other systems and across historical eras.

9. Lewis, *Abolition*, 60.

10. Ibid., 64.

11. Ibid., 65.

12. Ibid., 67. Lewis here anticipates the arguments of scientific naturalists such as E.

wrong with obeying our impulses/instincts? The problem, Lewis insists, is that "[o]ur instincts are at war ... Each instinct, if you listen to it, will claim to be gratified at the expense of the rest."[13] This need to satisfy our desires then proves destructive to us, Nature, and other humans. If left only up to our impulses/instincts, the weak are left to the mercy of the strong.

In "The Body and the Earth," Berry argues that we need to stop thinking of health as only the "absence of disease," and see instead that "the concept of health is rooted in the concept of wholeness."[14] In the same way, the purpose of a liberal arts education should be more than to secure a job and the "absence of poverty." Instead, a liberal arts education should strive for the health of wholeness, as we will discuss at the end of this chapter. Berry continues, "The word *health* belongs to a family of words, a listing of which will suggest how far the consideration of health must carry us: *heal, whole, wholesome, hale, hallow, holy* ... a definition to health that is positive and far more elaborate than that given by most medical doctors and the officers of public health."[15] Later he states, "Perhaps the fundamental damage of the specialist system—the damage from which all other damages issue—has been the isolation of the body."[16] The solution to this damage, for Berry, is healing via the restoration of connections. He explains: "Healing ... open[s] and restor[es] connections among the various parts—in this way restoring the ultimate simplicity of their union. When all the parts of the body are working together, are under each other's influence, we say that it is whole; it is healthy. The same is true of the world, of which our bodies are parts. The parts are healthy insofar as they are joined harmoniously to the whole."[17]

In the same way, literature that emphasizes these kinds of connections for health would benefit our students. The literature we teach our students could help them see and restore such connections in their own lives, thus

---

O. Wilson. Regarding Wilson's philosophy, Taylor states, "In his *On Human Nature*, the scientism has quite swallowed up the morality; indeed, we are offered a crassly reductive account of this latter. Natural selection wires in certain propensities to react, certain 'gut feelings', which are 'largely unconscious and irrational'" (*Sources*, 406). Taylor continues, "A reductive position of this sort is, of course, in a very deep sense untenable; that is, no one could actually live by it, and hence the best available account of what we actually live by cannot but be different" (406).

13. Lewis, *Abolition*, 36.
14. Berry, *Unsettling*, 103.
15. Ibid.
16. Ibid., 104.
17. Ibid., 110.

fostering healthy citizens within healthy communities. Berry sums up his argument by saying, "Only by restoring the broken connections can we be healed. Connection *is* health."[18] Here he makes a distinction between two types of work. He states, "There is work that is isolating, harsh, destructive, specialized or trivialized into meaninglessness. And there is work that is restorative, convivial, dignified and dignifying, and pleasing."[19] He calls this good work a "sacrament," because through it "we enact and understand our oneness with the Creation."[20] "Such work is unifying, healing," he says.[21] Likewise, the study of literature should be the type of work that is good in all of the ways that Berry lists. What such goods found in literature would help us towards this goal?

Earlier, we began with Bryson's three characteristics needed to confront issues in our modern culture: interdependence, humility, and skepticism. These ethical positions have their roots in what Taylor would call Judeo-Christian derived hypergoods. Remember, hypergoods are goods that give us a perspective to make sense of other goods and so they take priority in our hierarchy of values.[22] Three such hypergoods supplanted in modernism that Chesterton, Lewis, and Berry promote in their works are respectful engagement with tradition and family,[23] fidelity, and a belief in transcendence. It is through respectful engagement with tradition and family that we see the importance of interdependence and a skepticism towards technology that would undermine these foundational communities (of tradition and family). Likewise, belief in a transcendent order, a common group of values, fosters humility. Such belief includes acknowledgement of mystery and perhaps even miracles.[24] Also implied in humility is an acceptance of legitimate limits.

We will look first at how these authors emphasize respectful engagement with tradition and family in their writings. Chesterton considered the nuclear family to be the primary building block of society. For example, in *The Everlasting Man* he claims one of the first facts, "the thing that is

---

18. Ibid., 138.
19. Ibid.
20. Ibid.
21. Ibid., 140.
22. Taylor, *Sources of the Self*, 63.
23. This includes re-cognizing hierarchy in a more positive way.
24. Of course, there has been a long tradition of the discussion of miracles, but this topic is outside the scope of my argument.

before all thrones and even all commonwealths," is that of "the family."[25] He continues, "We can say that the family is the unit of the state; that it is the cell that makes up the formation. Round the family do indeed gather the sanctities that separate men from ants and bees. Decency is the curtain of that tent; liberty is the wall of that city; property is but the family farm; honour is but the family flag."[26] Here, Chesterton seems to say that many of our virtues in life do not come first and dictate how we are to treat families; rather, the respectful engagement with family comes first and our other virtues are the effect of this engagement. For Chesterton, the family unit consists of father, mother, and child and its three parts is no accident.[27] He therefore opposed any legislation from technocrats that encroached upon the basic rights of families. Like Chesterton, MacIntyre argues that our membership in our families and other communities precedes our pursuit of the good life and the virtues that enable us to do so. He states: "For I am never able to seek for the good or exercise the virtues only qua individual . . . I am someone's son or daughter, someone else's cousin or uncle . . . As such, I inherit from the past of my family, my city, my tribe, my nation, a variety of debts, inheritances, rightful expectations and obligations. These constitute the given of my life, my moral starting point."[28] The modern tendency, therefore, to impose universal legislation that upsets local family virtues and traditions is a false one, because the ethics held by legislators are not universal, formed in a vacuum, but are also derived from local family virtues and traditions.

In *The Flying Inn*, we can also see Chesterton emphasizing respectful engagement with tradition. The novel is permeated with instances of Mr. Pump and Patrick Dalroy reminiscing about people, places, and events that have happened throughout their traversing the English countryside. They often memorialize these local memories in song. In fact, the novel's numerous songs were collected separately in a later volume.[29] I believe Chesterton makes this reminiscing and memorializing such a prominent part of his novel because he values these traditions that bind the English people to-

---

25. Chesterton, *Everlasting*, 53.

26. Ibid., 54.

27. Steeped in his Catholicism, he states: "The old Trinity was of father and mother and child and is called the human family. The new is of child and mother and father and has the name of the Holy Family" (*Everlasting*, 55).

28. MacIntyre, *After Virtue*, 220.

29. Chesterton, *Wine, Water, and Song*.

gether regardless of time and class. He sets up the actions of Pump and Dalroy as a sharp contrast to the modern politician Ivywood who would turn his back on these traditions and customs for the sake of the latest fad. This transgression of Ivywood is exemplified most in the main plotline of the novel—his desire to abolish the sale of alcohol in inns and pubs in order to sober up the lower classes. For Chesterton, alcohol (used moderately, of course) is not just something that stands alone to be added to one's life or taken away at whim; rather, it is steeped in rituals and memories and traditions and to take it away would be to take away a part of the English peasants.

Like Chesterton, Lewis also emphasizes respectful engagement with family and tradition. In his appendix to *The Abolition of Man*, Lewis provides examples of eight virtues that have been shared by humans across time and cultures. His list includes Duties to Parents, Elders, and Ancestors and Duties to Children and Posterity. Using examples ranging from Greek, to Roman, to Egyptian, to Hindu, to Jewish, to Christian, he provides illustrations to support each virtue. For example, to illustrate Duties to Parents, Elders, and Ancestors, he cites the Hindu Janet as saying, "Your father is an image of the Lord of Creation, your mother an image of the Earth. For him who fails to honour them, every work of piety is in vain. This is the first duty," and the *Analects* of Ancient Chinese as saying, "When proper respect towards the dead is shown at the end and continued after they are far away, the moral force (*tê*) of a people has reached its highest point."[30] He provides these examples to support his idea of a *Tao*, or Truth, shared by the collective human race. We could consider these virtues/admonitions regarding family and tradition as a hypergood shared by humans across cultures and eras.

As for Chesterton, nuclear families (two parents and their children) do not feature prominently in Lewis's fiction. However, one place we can find Lewis emphasizing respectful engagement with family is in *That Hideous Strength*. The novel begins and ends by emphasizing the marriage of its protagonists, Jane and Mark Studdock. At the beginning of the novel, the newlyweds' marriage was cold and incomplete, because the two pursued their own interests as individuals (and academic intellectuals). However, they both learn by the end of the novel the importance of community, and they are reunited with their passion and humility for each other reignited. Besides this example, Lewis of course wrote the Narnia stories, which

---

30. Lewis, *Abolition*, 90–91.

feature and concern themselves with children, though the children are almost never with parents or parental figures. However, their close "familial" relation is clear. For example, in *The Lion, the Witch, and the Wardrobe*, Edmund accuses Susan of "Trying to talk like Mother" and Peter, acting like a father, scolds and bosses Edmund to the point that Edmund runs off to betray his siblings to the White Witch.[31] So we see, in the absence of their actual parents, the siblings working out their familial roles. Their closeness is especially made clear later when Peter defends his decision to rescue Edmund, saying "in a rather choking sort of voice": "All the same . . . we'd still have to go and look for him. He is our brother, after all, even if he is rather a little beast, and he's only a kid."[32] By the end of the novel, of course, the siblings find forgiveness and restoration (facilitated, of course, by Aslan) and their community is restored.

Berry's emphasis on tradition and family is prolific. One example we saw earlier: Jayber's acceptance of bachelorhood in Port William. When he accepted the job as barber in this community, he also accepted the tradition that went with it: barbers were bachelors and their shops were places for men to fraternize. Jayber could have gotten married, of course, but then he would have had to relinquish his traditional role, or membership, in the community as the facilitator of a particular arena of male society. Similarly, the Camp House in Port William was a zone of bachelorhood, owned first by Ernest Finley, then Burley Coulter, then Jayber Crow (after he retired). Another example of Berry's emphasis on respectful engagement with family can be seen in the life of Hannah Coulter. Though she is only married to her first husband, Virgil Feltner, for four years (he is killed in World War Two), she remains as a member of the Feltners, living in her in-law's house, until she remarries. As Hannah says, "I became one of the Feltners, and not in name only."[33] Here Berry is emphasizing a metaphysical change in Hannah's relationship, born out of a hypergood that respects the health of familial communities and will not divide what has been joined.

Second, all three authors treat fidelity as a hypergood. Berry states: "The idea of fidelity is perverted beyond redemption by understanding it as a grim, literal duty enforced only by willpower. This is the 'religious' insanity of making a victim of the body as a victory of the soul . . . It is reasonable

---

31. Lewis, *Lion*, 2.
32. Ibid., 81.
33. Berry, *Hannah*, 41.

to suppose, if fidelity is a virtue, that it is a virtue with a purpose. A purposeless virtue is a contradiction in terms."[34] He continues:

> Fidelity to human order, then, if it is fully responsible, implies fidelity also to natural order. Fidelity to human order makes devotion possible. Fidelity to natural order preserves the possibility of choice, the possibility of the renewal of devotion. Where there is no possibility of choice, there is no possibility of faith. One who returns home—to one's marriage and household and place in the world—desiring anew what was previously chosen, is neither the world's stranger nor its prisoner, but is at once in place and free.[35]

Fidelity seen as a hypergood, then, should emphasize the freedom gained by continually deciding to uphold a choice that does not exist in a vacuum. It should not be experienced as dutiful drudgery, as this way of looking at fidelity is individualistic and not communal (and therefore whole, or healthy).

This definition of fidelity that Berry offers here we of course saw earlier in our discussion of *Manalive*. Innocent Smith performed in his marriage what Berry calls "desiring anew what was previously chosen" in the unconventional but entirely faithful way he repeatedly wooed and "remarried" his wife. The significance of the hypergood Chesterton is emphasizing here is paramount. Unlike so many modern marriages that split up when the honeymoon period is over and the newness fades, the marriage that Smith acts out with his wife places fidelity first. It therefore dictates a return, rather than a departing, to the marriage vows. Chesterton's example in *Manalive* is not meant to naively imply that every marriage will be as romantically idealistic. Elsewhere Chesterton states, "Love is not blind; that is the last thing it is. Love is bound; and the more it is bound the less it is blind."[36] But whether or not the marriage is ideal is not the point; rather, if possible, the commitment to remaining in the place of one's marriage should supersede modern culture's messages to achieve one's individual highest potential. Like Berry, Chesterton's depiction of marriage privileges the wholeness of community, not utilitarian individualism.

For Lewis, his fiction does not prominently deal with marriages (except for *That Hideous Strength*, discussed above). However, we can see in his works and characters an emphasis on fidelity—choosing to stand by

---

34. Berry, *Unsettling*, 120–21.
35. Ibid., 130–31.
36. Chesterton, *Orthodoxy*, 101.

them no matter what. Perhaps one of the clearest examples can be seen in *Perelandra*. In this novel Ransom is sent on a mission from God to Venus in order to prevent that planet's "Eve" from being tempted by its "snake," the Un-Man. At one point in the novel Ransom realizes the only way to stop the Un-Man is to engage in physical combat with him and this (rightfully) terrifies him. He is tempted to abandon his mission: "Terrible follies came into his mind. He would fail to obey the Voice, but it would be all right because he would repent later on, when he was back on Earth. He would lose his nerve as St. Peter had done, and be, like St. Peter, forgiven."[37] Here Ransom is not only rationalizing excuses for abandoning his mission, but he is misusing Scripture to do so. Of course, Ransom resists these temptations and remains faithful to his mission, because he places fidelity to a higher-order good above his own personal comfort—an act that is the embodiment of Taylor's definition of a hypergood.

As we would imagine, Berry's fiction is full of examples of fidelity as a hypergood. We have already examined several instances. Earlier we saw how for Berry his return and commitment to the Camp paralleled his commitment in marriage to his wife. As he says in *The Long-Legged House*, his marriage is the center of his life and the Camp is the center of his marriage. Also, earlier we examined Jayber Crow's personal pledge of fidelity to Mattie, unique in that she could not reciprocate the pledge, but this does not keep Jayber from honoring it. Then, we saw in *Remembering* Andy's return home and his upholding fidelity to his wife, family, and physical/ancestral place. Here we will explore two new examples from Berry's fiction. The first demonstrates what can happen when a commitment to fidelity is forsaken, while the second provides an interesting twist on our understanding of fidelity.

For the first example, we turn to the novel *The Memory of Old Jack*. Written in 1974 (revised 1999), the novel depicts the last day of Jack Beechum's life. Set in 1952, Old Jack reflects on his life as he lounges about Port William on a hot September day. Before we see Jack's reflections on his past, we are given some perspective about a couple that lives on Mat Feltner's farm (a work in exchange for housing arraingment) that foreshadows the lack of fidelity explored later. The couple chooses not to invest their spare time in tending a garden or fattening a hog for the winter, but rather to spend each week fixing up their old car so it can take them into Hargrave (the nearest town). In other words, the couple chooses not to invest in their

---

37. Lewis, *Perelandra*, 125.

place any more than they have to, cheating on it in a sense as soon as they earn enough money. We are told of this couple: "Though the two of them live and work on the place [Mat's farm], they have no connection with it, no interest in it, no hope from it. They live, and appear content to live, from hand to mouth in the world of merchandise, connected to it by daily money poorly earned."[38]

Likewise, Jack's wife Ruth, we learn through his memories, grew up in the city and planned to bring him out of the country and into her city life. When it became clear to her that her vision was not his vision and that he was committed to his farm and place, she withheld herself from him, not only emotionally, but as much as possible, sexually. After Ruth gives birth to a stillborn son, "His presence was an invasion, a violation of the house. And except to eat and sleep, he began to stay away."[39] After this, Jack commits two infidelities. The first is in his desire for more land—the Ferrier place, which adjoined his farm. We are told:

> What he had in his mind now as he sat and thought, or walked the lengths of afternoons and thought, or worked and thought, was more land. He wanted more land. A man falling in his own esteem needs more ground under his feet; to stand again he may need the whole world for a foothold. His thoughts now ranged over the resources within his boundaries, and over the possibilities that lay outside them, seeking the terms of some new balance. His mind played over and over again the airy drama of ambition: how to use what he had to get what he wanted—a strange and difficult undertaking for him, who until then had wanted only what he had. Once he had hungered for the life his place could be made to yield. Now he would ask it to yield another place, at what expense to itself and to him he could not then have guessed.[40]

He therefore takes walks around the property. During one such walk we are told: "His trip over there that day had formalized a sort of betrothal; it had joined his vision to his will. Now his desire was no longer a dream; it was an intention . . . And now, having allowed desire to reach out beyond his own boundaries, he felt its exposure; he must rescue and preserve it and secure its triumph."[41] In his efforts to buy the property, "He was as ardent

---

38. Berry, *Memory*, 13.
39. Ibid., 49.
40. Ibid., 50.
41. Ibid., 55.

now in his cunning as he had ever been in love."[42] Also, "It was the first time in his life—and it was to be the last—that he ever resorted to stealth and deception, but he was pleased, for a while he was pleased, to discover he was good at it."[43] Eventually, he does buy the extra land, but it is too much for him to farm himself, and after three years he has to sell the farm to his rival at a heavy loss. Jack is back where he started, except with heavy debt: "The boundaries of the old farm, which he so confidently thought to surpass, now contain him like walls."[44]

Eventually, he commits a second infidelity—he begins an affair with a widow named Rose. With Rose, Jack finds a match for his passion, but eventually realizes he cannot give her what she needs—the stability of marriage and a family—because he is already married. We are told, "It was as though he bore for these two women the two halves of an irreparably divided love. With Ruth, his work had led to no good love. With Rose, his love led to no work."[45] Eventually, Rose is burned to death in a house fire. So, as with the Ferrier place, Jack's infidelities come at great cost to him. What Berry seems to be saying is that Jack's fidelity to his marriage and his place should have superseded his own personal desires. This message is not an easy one for modern ears. Of course, the best scenario would be if Jack had married Rose instead of Ruth. However, the possibility of divorce never enters into the story, possibly because of its taboo at the beginning of the twentieth century. Divorce, we might suppose, would also be a breach of fidelity and bring about its own consequences.

A second example of fidelity as a hypergood in Berry's fiction can be seen in the short story "Fidelity." Though from the title readers might suppose the story is about fidelity in marriage, the main plot of the story provides a much broader definition. Briefly, Nathan and Hannah Coulter and Danny and Lyda Branch, concerned about their Uncle Burley's health, take him to a hospital in Louisville. Shortly thereafter they regret their decision, as they realize the hospital will not release Burley until he improves or dies and, hooked up to machines, it is clear to them that he will not improve. Therefore, Danny sneaks into the hospital in the middle of the night and "kidnaps" Burley. He commits this "crime" in order to let Burley die in peace in the woods where he lived all his life near Port William. Danny

42. Ibid., 56.
43. Ibid.
44. Ibid., 69.
45. Ibid., 103.

digs a secret grave in the woods and buries Burley after he dies. Meanwhile, state patrol officer Detective Kyle Bode investigates Burley's kidnapping, but can find no evidence. The story ends with all of Burley's friends and family gathered in the Wheeler Catlett & Son law office (father and son who were also relatives of Burley's), showing Bode a true picture of fidelity.

The story presents a stark contrast between two ways of living—Bode's and Burley's family. Bode's family originated in Nowhere, Kentucky (fictionally placed just outside of Louisville) and his father insisted that he and his brother "get out of here and make something out of yourself."[46] After leaving home for the city "he married his high school sweetheart" and "became sexually liberated."[47] Humorously, we are told, "He suspected that his wife had experienced this liberation as well, but he did not catch her, and perhaps this was an ill omen for his police career."[48] Instead, she catches him with another woman but does not divorce him. However, "feel[ing] that she was limiting his development . . . he divorced her to be free to be himself."[49] He then remarries, but his second wife divorces him. It is here that Berry provides us with poignant insight to the modern epidemic of divorce that Bode represents:

> He knew that she had not left him because she was dissatisfied with him but because she was not able to be satisfied for very long with anything. He disliked and feared this in her at the same time that he recognized it in himself. He, too, was dissatisfied; he could not see what he had because he was always looking around for something else that he thought he wanted. And so perhaps it was out of mutual dissatisfaction that their divorce had come . . . They were all free, he supposed. But finally he had to ask if they were, any of them, better off . . . For they were not satisfied.[50]

This passage beautifully summarizes the problematic "freedom" found in modernity.[51] As we saw earlier in our discussion of Lewis, if moderns define freedom as permission to fulfill all of their desires, they will be dissatisfied

---

46. Berry, "Fidelity," 398.
47. Ibid.
48. Ibid.
49. Ibid., 398–99.
50. Ibid., 399.
51. See chapter 1, fn. 2 for Taylor's critique of Derrida and postmodernism on the issue of "untrammeled freedom," which Taylor labels the "least impressive side of modernism" (*Sources of the Self,* 489).

because those desires often are contradictory. In contrast, Berry presents his readers with a picture of orthodox fidelity, seen in the interconnected family tree of Burley's family. Bode cannot understand why anyone would choose to live in such an old-fashioned backwoods place, but we see that in his pursuit of happiness, defined as the freedom to make no permanent vows to any person or place, he has left himself alone, disconnected from the health of community.

A third hypergood emphasized by Chesterton, Lewis, and Berry is a belief in transcendence. There are two types of transcendence that must be distinguished: Transcendence (the mysterious separation between God and physical matter) and transcendence (the mysterious separation between physical matter). "transcendence," is a shadow of the Transcendent. One way they express this belief is through the action of "choosing." By choosing, I mean their characters are called to a task of some kind by a transcendent authority outside of themselves. Whether or not these characters want to perform these roles or tasks (and often they do not, or are at first reluctant), they do so anyway, acknowledging their places as parts of a greater transcendent whole. For Chesterton, Transcendence was a crucial component missing from paganism that Christianity provided, because "it divided God from the Cosmos."[52] It is no coincidence that the origins of the universe are described by orthodoxy as creation, because, says Chesterton, "All creation is separation. Birth is as solemn a parting as death."[53] He explains, "According to most philosophers, God in making the world enslaved it. According to Christianity, in making it, He set it free. God had written, not so much a poem, but rather a play; a play he had planned as perfect, but which had necessarily been left to human actors and stage-managers, who had since made a great mess of it."[54] Later Chesterton insists, "By insisting specially on the transcendence of God we get wonder, curiosity, moral and political adventure, righteous indignation—Christendom. Insisting that God is inside man, man is always inside himself. By insisting that God transcends man, man has transcended himself"[55] This paradox is the mysterious nature of the Incarnation.

Chesterton's emphasis on the importance of both Transcendence and transcendence is certainly evident in the novel *The Man Who Was Thursday*,

52. Chesterton, *Orthodoxy*, 112.
53. Ibid., 113.
54. Ibid.
55. Ibid., 204.

which he published around the same time as *Orthodoxy*.[56] The novel's protagonist, Gabriel Syme, is recruited—chosen—along with six others to be policemen for "The Last Crusade" by a mysterious man in a pitch black room. When Syme protests his lack of qualifications, saying, "I don't know of any profession of which mere willingness is the final test," the mysterious man replies: "I do . . . martyrs. I am condemning you to death. Good day."[57] All seven policemen, unbeknownst to each other, become members of a secret anarchists council led by a huge, ominous man called Sunday. The six policemen also assume the titles of days of the week, of which Syme becomes Thursday. One by one throughout the novel they discover each other to be policemen and eventually unite to take on Sunday. However, when confronted, Sunday stuns them with this: "There's one thing I'll tell you, though, about who I am. I am the man in the dark room, who made you all policemen."[58] So, very confusingly for both the policemen and readers, the same person recruited for the purposes of both good and evil. Syme eventually understands why, exclaiming: "Listen to me . . . Shall I tell you the secret of the whole world? It is that we have only known the back of the world. We see everything from behind, and it looks brutal . . . Cannot you see that everything is stooping and hiding a face? If we could only get round in front—."[59] Here it seems to me that Chesterton is describing the confusion humans experience when we consider ourselves in relation to nature. We all experience birth, which is the separation of ourselves from what is around us. So we see things from the back. Chesterton is challenging us to see what lies behind Nature—the Transcendent creator God, or the key that unlocks the mystery faced by the pagans and philosophers described in *Orthodoxy*. This reading helps to explain why, after awaking from his vision or dream, "Syme's state of mind is clearly identifiable as that peculiar

---

56. We must keep in mind that this novel is subtitled *A Nightmare*, and it is certainly fantastical, as Chesterton himself even had to remind his readers as late as 1936: "The book was called *The Man Who Was Thursday: A Nightmare*. It was not intended to describe the real world as it was, or as I thought it was, even when my thoughts were considerably less settled than they are now. It was intended to describe the world of wild doubt and despair which the pessimists were generally describing at that date; with just a gleam of hope in some double meaning of doubt, which even the pessimists felt in some fitful passion" (Chesterton, *Man*, 186).

57. Chesterton, *Man*, 48–49.

58. Ibid., 155.

59. Ibid., 170.

WHOLENESS, THE HUMANITIES, AND PLACE

to religious conversion."[60] Syme has come to understand the importance of transcendence to the human condition and this helps him metaphorically see things from "round in front" or, in other words, to see the Transcendent behind Nature.

Likewise, Lewis's characters experience callings from the Transcendent numerous times in his fiction. In *Out of the Silent Planet*, I do not think readers are supposed to see Ransom's journey to Malacandra as chance. Instead of taking a mentally challenged boy to offer as a sacrifice to the "aliens" they encountered on Malacandra, Weston and Devine instead take Ransom, a philologist who can quickly learn the languages of the three species on that strange planet. The Oyarsa [archangel] of Malacandra affirms this near the end, saying to Ransom, "[I]t is not without the wisdom of Maleldil [Christ] that we have met now and I have learned so much of your world."[61] In *Perelandra* this transcendent purpose for Ransom is made even clearer, as Ransom realizes: "One of the purposes for which He had done all this was to save Perelandra not through Himself but through Himself in Ransom."[62] Soon after he reasons:

> The pattern is so large that within the little frame of earthly experience there appear pieces of it between which we can see no connection, and other pieces between which we can . . . Before his Mother had born him, before his ancestors had been called Ransoms, before *ransom* had been the name for a payment that delivers, before the world was made, all these things had so stood together in eternity that the very significance of the pattern at this point lay in their coming together in just this fashion. And he bowed his head and groaned and repined against his fate—to be still a man and yet to be forced up into the metaphysical world, to enact what philosophy only thinks.[63]

Lewis then reaffirms the importance of the transcendent at the end of the novel, when Ransom has a vision of the Great Dance. We see that Ransom is not the center of the universe, but rather part of an intricate web of connections, set in place by the Transcendent. By accepting his place in this larger community, he finds peace and health.

---

60. Oddie, *Chesterton*, 332.
61. Lewis, *Out*, 142.
62. Lewis, *Perelandra*, 123.
63. Ibid., 125.

A belief in transcendence is also demonstrated time and again throughout the *Chronicles of Narnia*. One of the clearest examples comes at the end of *The Horse and His Boy*. King Lune has two sons, Corin and Cor. Cor, the eldest, is to be Lune's rightful heir, but he does not want the responsibility. So the two have this brief exchange:

> "But I don't want it," said Cor. "I'd far rather—"
> "'Tis no question what thou wantest, Cor, nor I either. 'Tis in course of law." . . .
> "But, Father, couldn't you make whichever you like to be the next King?"
> "No. The King's under the law, for it's the law makes him a king. Hast no more power to start away from thy crown than any sentry from his post."[64]

Here Lewis is clearly demonstrating that even for kings, who we would expect to be at the top of any hierarchy, there are external, transcendent goods higher than them to which they must hold. The law precedes the law-enforcer.[65] This principle reminds us of what Lewis said earlier in this chapter from *The Abolition of Man*: teachers and students alike are subject to the *Tao* and therefore teachers cannot teach students differently from how the *Tao* prescribes.

For Berry, this belief in a transcendent choosing informs his fiction. In his short novel *Remembering*, the beginning of chapter 4 (titled "A Long Choosing") explores this belief in Andy's thoughts:

> That he [Andy] is who he is and no one else is the result of a long choosing, chosen and chosen again. He thinks of the long dance of men and women behind him, most of whom he never knew . . . who, choosing one another, chose him. He thinks of the choices, too, by which he chose himself as he now is . . . He knows that some who might have left chose to stay, and that some who did leave chose to return, and he is one of them. Those choices have formed in time and place the pattern of a membership that chose

---

64. Lewis, *Horse*, 214–15.

65. Similarly, in J. R. R. Tolkien's *The Lord of the Rings* we find characters chosen for roles to which they must hold. For example, Frodo is "chosen" by the transcendent for the task of taking the Ring to Mount Doom. As Elrond tells him, "I think that this task is appointed for you, Frodo; and that if you do not find a way, no one will" (Tolkien, *Fellowship*, 264). Neither Gandalf, nor Elrond, nor any other authority figure forces Frodo to complete his task—Frodo chooses to do the task and then the others affirm this transcendent calling.

him, yet left him free until he should choose it, which he did once, and now has done again.⁶⁶

In this example, we see that Andy's life was influenced by numerous choices that were outside of his control, many of which happened even before he was born. Because of these external choices, he has been born into the membership of a specific community and he realizes that he has the opportunity to make choices of his own that will affect others. MacIntyre states, "What I am, therefore, is in key part what I inherit, a specific past that is present to some degree in my present. I find myself part of a history and that is generally to say, whether I like it or not, whether I recognize it or not, one of the bearers of a tradition."⁶⁷ When referring to his own biography, Berry often uses the same term, "inheritance." Referring to his home (the Camp), he states, "[T]here is a sense in which my own life is inseparable from the history and the place. It is a complex inheritance, and I have been both enriched and bewildered by it."⁶⁸ What Andy, MacIntyre, and Berry all seem to share is an acceptance of a transcendent inheritance that informs their quest for health, or wholeness. In other words, the land outlives them (and by extension, us) and they are chosen as caretakers for a time. This phenomenon is transcendent because of the acknowledgment by these individuals of a larger, mysterious existence that lays claim to them beyond their physical human experience.

Of course, a byproduct of accepting one's chosen-ness by the transcendent to be a part of a community is also accepting the limits membership in said community imposes. It is difficult for our modern eyes to see limits as positive. We live in a world that does not want to hear such a message, a world that sees limits as chains keeping us from our full potential or progress. However, as Goethe says: "Mastery is revealed in limitation / And law alone can set us free again."⁶⁹ We can see instances of this paradox all around us. For example, to get in shape a person must choose to accept the limits such a process would entail: limiting the amount and type of foods consumed, limiting the amount of lethargy allowed, and limiting the amount of time one stays awake in order to get enough rest. These limits may not always be easy or fun to abide by, but living within them allows the person to be healthier. A popular weight loss program, with its daily point

66. Berry, *Remembering*, 169.
67. MacIntyre, *After Virtue*, 221.
68. Berry, *Long-Legged*, 171.
69. Goethe, "Nature," 125–26, lines 13–14.

limits, is a great example of this principle. Likewise, our laws and regulations for how to operate automobiles on roads allow us to drive our cars with peace of mind, not paralyzed in the fear of what to do or what other motorists around us will do. I can freely drive through an intersection with a green light, knowing that the other motorists will stop at their red lights. In these instances, though, our freedom is determined by our obedience, and others' obedience, to these limits.

Likewise, for Chesterton, the limits to places, ethics, and things, are interconnected. For him, limits also created a paradox: by accepting them we enlarge, not shrink, our lives. He uses as his prime example fairy tales, in which the magic in the story always hung on a command, or limit. For example, Cinderella could go to the ball, but she must be home by midnight.[70] Or, for artists, the frame of a canvas or the structure of a sonnet is not viewed as limits to begrudgingly obeyed, but fun challenges in which artists choose to operate. Chesterton states, "The artist loves his limitations: they constitute the *thing* he is doing. The painter is glad that the canvas is flat. The sculptor is glad that the clay is colourless."[71]

Furthermore, limits are the key intersection between ethics, places, and things. As Chesterton points out in *Orthodoxy*, we must impose limits in order to love things. For example, he says, "I could never mix in the common murmur of that rising generation against monogamy, because no restriction on sex seemed so odd and unexpected as sex itself . . . To complain that I could only be married once was like complaining that I had only been born once . . . It showed, not an exaggerated sensibility to sex, but a curious insensibility to it . . . Polygamy is a lack of the realization of sex; it is like a man plucking five pears in mere absence of mind."[72] In other words, to hold one's spouse separate from all others is to value him or her. In the same way, holding to one place and rejecting all others demonstrates its value. In contrast, when humans move from lover to lover, or place to place, in the name of living life to its fullest, they find that they in fact devalue those things and do not experience the fullness of life that comes from limits and devotion.

Lewis makes a similar point more than once in his writings. In *Perelandra*, Ransom reflects on this principle of limits regarding appetite when he has his first taste of the fruit on that strange planet. The fruit tastes unlike

70. Chesterton, *Orthodoxy*, 77.
71. Ibid., 52.
72. Ibid., 79–80.

anything on earth and is so good he thinks "wars would be fought and nations betrayed" for just one sip.⁷³ Finishing one fruit, Ransom reaches for another, but then hesitates:

> As he let the empty gourd fall from his hand and was about to pluck a second one, it came into his head that he was now neither hungry nor thirsty. And yet to repeat a pleasure so intense and almost so spiritual seemed an obvious thing to do. His reason, or what we commonly take to be reason in our own world, was all in favour of tasting this miracle again; the childlike innocence of fruit, the labours he had undergone, the uncertainty of the future, all seemed to commend the action. Yet something seemed opposed to this "reason." It is difficult to suppose that this opposition came from desire, for what desire would turn from so much deliciousness? But for whatever cause, it appeared to him better not to taste again. Perhaps the experience had been so complete that repetition would be a vulgarity—like asking to hear the same symphony twice in a day.
>
> As he stood pondering over this and wondering how often in his life on earth he had reiterated pleasures not through desire, but in the teeth of desire and in obedience to a spurious rationalism, he noticed that the light was changing.⁷⁴

Ransom's dilemma is an example of the "hyperrationality" that is part of Bryson's definition of modern culture, above. As he was a highly educated academic, we can assume this hyperrationality would have been a product of Ransom's education. Ordinarily, we think of "the humanities" as a place of "liberation" ("liberal arts"). Here, however, Lewis suggests such rational thinking can lead us astray if it is not checked by particular concerns for what is best.

Another obvious way limits are a valuable corrective to our modern culture is in the way they help temper our proclivity to consumption. As we have seen, Chesterton, Berry, and to some degree Lewis, all provide valuable contributions to discussions of economics. Their words are a corrective to the materialism and waste of our age. Arendt argues, "[T]he spare time of the *animal laborans* is never spent in anything but consumption, and the more time left to him, the greedier and more craving his appetites ... so that consumption is no longer restricted to the necessities but ... on the superfluities of life" creating "the grave danger that eventually no object

---

73. Lewis, *Perelandra*, 37.
74. Ibid., 37–38.

of the world will be safe from consumption and annihilation through consumption."[75] She continues, "One of the obvious danger signs that we may be on our way to bring into existence the ideal of the *animal laborans* is the extent to which our whole economy has become a waste economy, in which things must be almost as quickly devoured and discarded as they have appeared in the world."[76] Who can deny that her warning has come about? In America, for example, tractor-trailers haul trash from our cities out to dump them in our rural areas, even cross-state. Even though manufacturers are increasingly packaging things in recyclable material, their products and packaging are still consumable and disposable. Our status as *animal laborans* stands.

Of course, this transformation into *animal laborans* could not have come about so quickly without our advancements and reliance on technology. In fact, a key component to our consumerism is our acceptance and use of technology and the industrial system. As we saw earlier, Chesterton, Lewis, and Berry remind us that the use of technology often comes at a price to our humanity. Also, to think and speak so looks foolish and backwards to moderns. In *What Are People For?* Berry states:

> I realize that, by now, my argument has crossed a boundary line of which everyone in our 'realistic' society is keenly aware. I will be perceived to have crossed over into 'utopianism' or fantasy. Unless I take measures to prevent it, I am going to hear somebody say, 'All that would be very nice, if it were possible. Can't you be realistic?' ... To me, an economy that sees the life of a community or a place as expendable, and reckons its value only in terms of money, is not acceptable because it is *not* realistic. I am thinking as I believe we must think if we wish to discuss the *best* uses of people, places, and things, and if we wish to give affection some standing in our thoughts.[77]

Here Berry offers an important distinction: the goal is not to eliminate consumption altogether—this is impossible—but to check our consumption by making it subservient to issues of what is best for places, people, and things. Of course, we are not going to able to do so if we continue to see things as individual parts, not an interconnected whole. In *The Unsettling of America*, Berry states in the chapter titled "The Ecological Crisis is a Crisis

75. Arendt, *Human*, 133.
76. Ibid., 134.
77. Berry, "Argument," 113.

of Character," "The disease of the modern character is specialization."[78] He explains:

> Looked at from the standpoint of the social *system*, the aim of specialization may seem desirable enough. The aim is to see that the responsibilities of government, law, medicine, engineering, agriculture, education, etc., are given into the hands of the most skilled, best prepared people. The difficulties do not appear until we look at specialization from the opposite standpoint—that of individual persons. We then begin to see the grotesquery—indeed, the impossibility—of an idea of community wholeness that divorces itself from any idea of personal wholeness.[79]

He adds, "The supposedly fortunate citizen is therefore left with only two concerns: making money and entertaining himself."[80] And of course, technology in modern media is such that we will never get this satisfaction. There is always "one more thing" to stay tuned in to see, keeping us distracted from a deeper anxiety. Here "anxiety" is similar to the dissatisfaction of "desire" discussed earlier. Berry states, "He [the average citizen] ought to be anxious, because he is helpless. That he is dependent upon so many specialists, the beneficiary of so much expert help, can only mean that he is a captive, a potential victim."[81] Of course, we want our students to be better than average citizens and one of the primary reasons we teach the humanities is to help our students see themselves and their world within a larger whole. It is important, therefore, that our students study authors whose works help them recognize and resist this dependency on specialists, in order that they might find wholeness and health for themselves and their communities.

It is the way Chesterton, Lewis, and Berry dramatize the interaction of these hypergoods that makes study of their works the ideal way to understand and approach personal wholeness. As indicated earlier, this personal wholeness means more than self-preservation and self-assertion. In order to be whole, humans need to have a proper relation to places, ethics, and things. As we have seen, Chesterton, Lewis, and Berry can help us experience a more communal, interdependent form of personal wholeness through the reading and discussing of their works. Personal wholeness, after all, is the goal of the humanities. These three authors enable us to

---

78. Berry, *Unsettling*, 19.
79. Ibid.
80. Ibid., 20.
81. Ibid., 21.

read their fiction and creative non-fiction[82] and "live out" these hypergoods in their characters. We do not just experience these hypergoods through them, but we see how rich the world really is. Unlike many of their contemporaries, these authors emphasize the productive, not merely the evil, parts of the world.

First, though, we need to eliminate the false notion that our modern age has somehow progressed beyond the hypergoods of past ages. In *Orthodoxy*, Chesterton states, "We often hear it said, for instance, 'What is right in one age is wrong in another.' This is quite reasonable, if it means that there is a fixed aim, and that certain methods attain at certain times and not at other times."[83] With his typical humor, Chesterton underscores the irony inherent in the belief that ethics change between time periods: "[T]his idea of a fundamental alteration in the standard is one of the things that make thought about the past or future simply impossible. The theory of a complete change of standards in human history does not merely deprive us of the pleasure of honouring our fathers; it deprives us even of the more modern and aristocratic pleasure of despising them."[84] We need to recognize that perhaps the perceived changes in our ethics are not the pursuit of some new ideal, but rather the deviation from an old ideal that has never been replaced. Our hypergoods, therefore, are consistent across eras, and we should study modern literature that reflects this consistency. In chapter 3 we read Berry's assertion that stories in the humanities should not be taught as artifacts, because the same external set of values should be shared. As such, I believe the writings of Chesterton, Lewis, and Berry tackle many of the key issues of any time, especially respectful engagement with tradition and family, fidelity, and belief in transcendence, and they must be included in the canon of the humanities.

For example, when the characters in Chesterton's works do unconventional, seemingly crazy actions that turn out to be quite reasonable once they are explained, readers are forced to confront the modern narratives (and hypergoods) that they conform to without question. In other words, Chesterton uses the unconventional in his works to underscore the importance (taken lightly by moderns) of the conventions (hypergoods) that tradition has upheld. Innocent Smith is an excellent example of this

---

82. And their poetry, especially in the case of Berry, though this genre is outside the scope of this volume.

83. Chesterton, *Orthodoxy*, 44.

84. Ibid., 45.

paradoxical way of living—he does not sit around fragmented like the members of Beacon House, but rather lives exuberantly and freely in his beliefs in tradition, family, fidelity, and transcendence. His actions seem unconventional (and illegal), but are actually truer to the hypergoods than the actions of the other characters.

In Lewis we see much of the same. In both the *Space Trilogy* and *Chronicles of Narnia,* his protagonists recognize the importance of tradition, family, fidelity, and transcendence, ordering their lives accordingly and living in the freedom circumscribed by these hypergoods. For example, when Edmund betrays his siblings in obedience to his natural desire for Turkish Delight, he transgresses the hypergood of respectful engagement with family and therefore severs himself from community. As a consequence, his health (wholeness) suffers in the White Witch's palace until he repents and is accepted back into his familial (and Narnian) community. In recognizing that they cannot find wholeness in tackling their problems or seeking their desires as individuals, Lewis's protagonists find their identity in community, whether of friends, family, or a shared belief in the transcendent (whether Aslan or Maleldil).

Likewise, Berry's writings affirm the same message. When his characters choose to acknowledge the hypergoods of respectful engagement with tradition and family, fidelity, and transcendence, they include themselves in larger human, natural, and metaphysical communities. This choosing to be a part of a larger community makes his characters whole, bringing them peace and contentment. We saw a strong example of this earlier in *Remembering.* The novel's title implies this reconnection to wholeness—Andy chooses to turn from his personal desires of self-fulfillment and return to his family and community. He chooses to adhere to the three hypergoods we have discussed and therefore becomes whole again, re-membering himself to the traditional, familial, natural, and metaphysical things he had severed.

Taken together, these three hypergoods help to restore the connections between individuals and other people, places, and things. These restored connections create health for the community, a health measured by wholeness—both for the individuals and for the community. Respectful engagement with tradition and family forges connections to past, present, and future generations. It allows us to respect not only the cultural values of our human communities, but also the natural environment as well, because it is the inheritance of future generations. Fidelity forges connections between people in marriages, friendships, work, and family bonds. It also forges connections between humans and their natural environment—our commitment fosters our love. Finally, belief in transcendence forges connections between humans and other humans, places, and things by fostering humility in us, a humility that allows us to put our own self-interests aside for the health of the greater community. Working together, the overall health or wholeness of the community allows for the health and wholeness of the parts, human and otherwise, that make up the community. Reading and studying authors such as Chesterton, Lewis, and Berry helps us to see the importance of these hypergoods to the health of our communities, and ourselves, and therefore their inclusion in the humanities is paramount.

In fact, in teaching these authors I would encourage my students to see in these authors' characters the "embodiment" of this "wholeness" that is the humanities, primarily in two ways. First, their characters are not acted upon, but, as we have seen, are actors who recognize their *telos*. So much of modern literature is full of protagonists who find themselves powerless to act and are therefore tragic because they cannot help being acted upon. This literature, of course, echoes a feeling that we moderns do tend to feel on a day-to-day basis—our government, our employers, our creditors, our family and friends, among others, all act upon us. For our students this is no different. However, the characters in the fiction of Chesterton, Lewis, and Berry are determined to act appropriate to their *telos*, regardless of what it might cost them, because they see themselves as part of a bigger story that has been defined for them. And so in Chesterton characters see themselves as part of an English and orthodox tradition, in Lewis characters are a part of the Great Dance, and in Berry characters are part of a "membership."

Second, their characters are not individualistic, but characters who see themselves as part of a larger community. In contrast to the self-made modern human that is so popular (rags to riches stories), the characters in Chesterton, Lewis, and Berry recognize that they need to rely on others to help inform their identities and actions. Their characters are not afraid to ask for help or give help, when appropriate. As a result, they recognize that the health of their community is just as important as their own personal well-being. And so in Chesterton characters risk imprisonment and death to protect their local communities and customs, in Lewis characters sacrifice for one another, and in Berry neighbors pitch in to help each other with their farm work. All three authors draw us to the possibility of personal wholeness found in looking past our individualism and seeing the world as inter-connected and inter-dependent. Their fiction offers therefore a rich and powerful addition to the humanities.

CONCLUSION

By way of conclusion, I would like to assert that the hypergood acting as the impetus behind the returns of Chesterton, Lewis, and Berry to place is grace. According to *Oxford Dictionaries*, the word "grace" is derived from "Middle English: via Old French from Latin *gratia*, from *gratus* 'pleasing, thankful'; related to grateful."[1] Later, the term took on a more theological meaning of "a totally gratuitous gift [from God] on which man has absolutely no claim."[2] As we can see, the definition of grace has two important components. First, there is an unmerited action whereby one entity gives a gift to another. Second, there is in the gift-receiver a response of gratefulness for the gift. In addition, we can see that "grace" is rooted in the particular—a gift. Certainly we can see this in the Judeo-Christian tradition. For example, David writes in the Psalms:

> 9 Thou visitest the earth, and waterest it: thou greatly enrichest it with the river of God, which is full of water: thou preparest them corn, when thou hast so provided for it.
>
> 10 Thou waterest the ridges thereof abundantly: thou settlest the furrows thereof: thou makest it soft with showers: thou blessest the springing thereof.
>
> 11 Thou crownest the year with thy goodness; and thy paths drop fatness.
>
> 12 They drop upon the pastures of the wilderness: and the little hills rejoice on every side.
>
> 13 The pastures are clothed with flocks; the valleys also are covered over with corn; they shout for joy, they also sing.[3]

1. *Oxford Dictionaries*, s.v. "grace," http://www.oxforddictionaries.com/.
2. *Modern Catholic Dictionary*, s.v. "grace," by Fr. John Hardon, http://www.catholicculture.org/.
3. Ps 65:9–13 (King James Version).

We see clearly in this passage the practice of grace: God providing gifts to the land (and by extension, his people) and the land (and people) being grateful in return. How were they to be grateful? They were to demonstrate their gratefulness by extending grace to others: "Is not this the fast that I have chosen? to loose the bands of wickedness, to undo the heavy burdens, and to let the oppressed go free, and that ye break every yoke? Is it not to deal thy bread to the hungry, and that thou bring the poor that are cast out to thy house? when thou seest the naked, that thou cover him; and that thou hide not thyself from thine own flesh?"[4] Clearly God expected his people to extend grace to others—give gifts to those who do not merit them.

Chesterton, Lewis, and Berry are all aware of this Judeo-Christian connection between grace and particularities and places. Through their writings we can distinguish the two types of grace described above: everyday "grace" (among creation) and spiritual "Grace" (between God and creation). What follows are some brief examples of this awareness in their writings.

From "the autumn of 1894 to late 1896," Chesterton kept a notebook full of ideas, including poems.[5] About this notebook Oddie states, "But The Notebook's most powerful theme, insistently returned to again and again, is his gratitude for everything in his life."[6] Oddie then quotes a representative poem concerning Chesterton's gratitude from The Notebook:

> You say grace before meals,
> All right
> But I say grace before the play and the opera,
> And grace before the concert and the pantomime,
> And grace before I open a book,
> And grace before sketching, painting,
> Swimming, fencing, boxing, walking, playing, dancing;
> And grace before I dip the pen in the ink.[7]

Here we can see quite clearly that for Chesterton grace was more than the more recent, limiting definition of a prayer before meals. Instead, we see that he understood Grace as gratefulness for every aspect of life—an

---

4. Isa 58:6–7 (King James Version).
5. Oddie, *Chesterton*, 145.
6. Ibid., 150.
7. Ibid.

attitude that acknowledges the gift giver. Decades later, Chesterton writes elsewhere, "I do not, in my private capacity, believe that a baby gets his best physical food by sucking his thumb; nor that a man gets his best moral food by sucking his soul, and denying its dependence on God or other good things. I would maintain that thanks are the highest form of thought; and that gratitude is happiness doubled by wonder."[8] He calls this practiced grace "faith in receptiveness" and "respect for things outside oneself."[9] Here we see that Chesterton finds a direct connection between a life of gratitude (grace) and valuing others. The connection lies in the humility required to accept an unmerited gift, because we recognize that we share the same lack of merit as others.

Likewise, Lewis understood the importance of grace, especially in how it shapes our understanding of others. In an interview with the actor and narrator Max McLean, Lewis's stepson Douglas Gresham tells an insightful story regarding Lewis and grace. Once, Gresham says, some academics were arguing in the common room at Oxford about what one main thing separated Christianity from all other major religions. Lewis walked into the room (possibly to get a pint of beer, Gresham surmises) and the academics deferred to his opinion on the matter. Lewis said, "Well, that's easy, that's grace." Gresham finishes his story by saying, "The undeserved love of God for man is what separates Christianity from all other faiths."[10] Lewis also writes about Grace later in his life, linking it to Charity, one of the four loves, in his book of the same title. He distinguishes between the two types I outlined earlier: Grace and grace. He says, "That such a Gift-love comes by Grace and should be called Charity, everyone will agree. But I have to add something which will not perhaps be so easily admitted. God, as it seems to me, bestows two other gifts; a supernatural Need-love of Himself and a supernatural Need-love of one another."[11] He adds, "What is stranger still is that He creates in us a more than natural receptivity of Charity from our fellow-men. Need is so near greed and we are so greedy already that it seems a strange grace. But I cannot get it out of my head that this is what happens."[12] Lewis is making a distinction between the Grace that humans accept from God (and realize their dependence upon) and

8. Chesterton, *Short History*, 59.
9. Ibid.
10. Gresham, "Interview."
11. Lewis, *Four Loves*, 129.
12. Ibid.

the grace that humans accept from each other (and also realize their, God-created of course, dependence upon). Grace, for Lewis, works itself out in a process: "Thus God, admitted to the human heart, transforms not only Gift-love but Need-love; not only our Need-love of Him, but our Need-love of one another."[13]

Finally, we see in Berry's poetry an explicit understanding between place and grace. In "The Peace of Wild Things," Berry writes: "For a time / I rest in the grace of the world, and am free."[14] In "The Gift of Gravity," Berry writes:

> We are what we are given
> and what is taken away;
> blessed be the name
> of the given and taker.
> For everything that comes
> is a gift, the meaning always
> carried out of sight
> to renew our whereabouts,
> always a starting place.
> And every gift is perfect
> in its beginning, for it
> is "from above, and cometh down
> from the Father of lights."
> Gravity is grace.[15]

Likewise, we see here that Berry understands Grace through the metaphor of gravity: just as everything falls through gravity, all of creation has fallen as a gift from God. This acknowledgement of grace has for Berry as serious obligation: to treat creation with respect and to care for it. He ends the poem thus: "This grace is gravity."

This relationship between grace and Grace seems implicit in the writings of Chesterton, Lewis, and Berry. The experienced (and practiced) grace on earth is a shadow of the transcendent Grace these authors acknowledged. For instance, just as in Lewis's writings heaven is a perfected form of what we experience now, the grace we have now points to the perfected

---

13. Ibid., 133.
14. Lines 10–11.
15. Lines 11–24.

CONCLUSION

Grace. To acknowledge the importance of grace may seem strange to moderns. Our society is all about the value of justice (as long as we're talking about others, not ourselves), but sees grace as weakness. Of the two, however, grace requires more strength, because in restoring their relationship individuals must set aside their differences out of respect for the health of the community. This grace acknowledges an external communal good—community wholeness—just as Grace acknowledges an external communal Good—physical and metaphysical wholeness. In other words, both grace and Grace restore wholeness to communities, making them healthy. In chapter 4, we saw that Berry describes health as "wholeness."[16]

Grace can be considered the quintessence of the hypergoods. It requires humility, acknowledges community (wholeness), and promotes health. Grace, therefore, should be valued in the humanities, and including these authors can allow us to better recognize the particularities—to stop and smell the roses, so to speak. Emphasizing particularities is an essential corrective to the issue of utilitarian "instrumentalism" we discussed in chapter 3, exemplified by Narnia's Queen Jadis and Uncle Andrew.[17] These characters saw people, places, and things as "subjects" or "raw material" to be used up—abstractions, rather than particulars.

As we have seen in their biographies in chapter 1, grace played an essential role in helping Chesterton, Lewis, and Berry return home to their faith. For example, in chapter 1 we saw Berry say of his questions, "[T]hey are spoken in reverence for the order and grace that I see, and that I trust beyond my power to see."[18] Grace as a value can also be seen throughout their writings, and in closing we will look at a new, summative example from each author of the kind of grace that, when "incarnated" in stories, poems, or reflective prose, can give new life and significance to the study of the humanities.

For our example of grace in Chesterton's writings, we turn to Father Brown. Perhaps more than any other character, Father Brown best embodies the spirit of Chesterton, and that is why he is the best known of Chesterton's characters. Chesterton wrote his Father Brown detective stories over a long period of time, from 1910 to 1935. Much more than a sleuth, Father Brown offered insight into the soul, not just the psyche, of humans. In several cases, Father Brown would, after getting a confession from the

---

16. See pages 103–4.
17. See pages 87–90.
18. Berry, *Long-Legged*, 200.

guilty party, let him or her go (if the crime was of a spiritual, rather than a legal nature). In an early story of this kind, Chesterton provides a clear picture of grace. In "The Queer Feet," Father Brown catches the thief of some silver from a dinner party and, after the thief repents and returns the silver, he lets the thief go. When later asked if he caught the criminal, Father Brown replies: "Yes ... I caught him, with an unseen hook and an invisible line which is long enough to let him wander to the ends of the world, and still to bring him back with a twitch upon the thread."[19] Evelyn Waugh later borrowed this line to title the third book of *Brideshead Revisited*: "A Twitch Upon the Thread." In the novel, Cordelia makes this speech:

> D'you know what papa said when he became a Catholic? Mummy told me once. He said to her: 'You have brought back my family to the faith of their ancestors' ... [T]he family haven't been very constant, have they? There's him gone and Sebastian gone and Julia gone. But God won't let them go for long, you know. I wonder if you remember the story mummy read us ... 'Father Brown' said something like 'I caught him' (the thief) 'with an unseen hook ...'[20]

Terry Teachout says of this passage: "Chesterton's metaphor, so placed, announces the inmost theme of *Brideshead*; and, in a nutshell, it also manages to suggest all the poetry and spiritual depth of the Father Brown stories themselves."[21] Chesterton's stories remind us that we are never far from grace ourselves, so we should therefore extend grace to others. Such a focus is communal, not individualistic. Father Brown is a great exemplar for education, because he solves his cases with a strict adherence to reason, though this reason is as spiritual as it is scientific. That is, Father Brown's reasoning is more holistic.

Similarly, Lewis's fascination with grace was long-standing. As a young man, pre-conversion, he was struck by the beauty of the story of Cupid and Psyche, as told by Petronius in *The Golden Ass*, and he had a desire to retell the story. He finally did so, as the last work of fiction he wrote before his death: *Till We Have Faces*. His novel is told from the perspective of Orual, the eldest sister to Psyche who is jealous of her beauty. At the very end of the novel, Orual experiences a vision whereby she sees that she is one of a number of temptations Psyche has had to resist in order to obey the divine

---

19. Chesterton, "The Queer Feet," 50.
20. Waugh, *Brideshead*, 200.
21. Teachout, "A Twitch," 1231.

command given to her. Orual repents, telling Psyche: "Never again will I call you mine; but all there is of me shall be yours. Alas, you know now what it's worth. I never wished you well, never had one selfless thought of you. I was a craver."[22] After this repentance, Orual is told by "a great voice" (God), "You also are Psyche."[23] Orual's experience here with grace changes her and allows her to see her past from a new perspective, especially how she had been living for the wrong things. She was "craver," a consumer, obsessed with the wrong values. However, her repentance, which allowed her to accept grace, restored health—wholeness—once again to her immediate relationship with her sister and also her larger community.

Turning to Berry, perhaps one of the best grace-filled stories in his canon is his recent novel *Hannah Coulter*. The novel is unique in that it is the only one of Berry's "autobiographic" stories told from the perspective of a woman. Hannah begins her tale by saying, "This is my story, my giving of thanks."[24] This statement sets the grace-filled tone of the narrative, as "giving of thanks" is analogous with being grateful. To be certain, Hannah's life has its share of miseries: her mother dies when she is a child and her stepmom is cruel to her, her first husband dies in WWII, her children all move away when they grow up, and she outlives her second husband. Through each tragedy, though, she maintains a humility forged by grace that allows her to respect her enemies and her community. She remains aware that her story is interconnected with those of others, whose stories have value too. She therefore focuses on the positives: a grandmother who with grace shields her from her stepmom, her first husband's in-laws who with grace care for her when he dies, and a long, fruitful marriage by Grace to her second husband. Eventually, she even extends grace in the form of forgiveness to her stepmom and has the opportunity to receive with grace and open arms a prodigal son who leaves a reckless life of drugs and returns home. She is able to act this way towards others, to be an active agent for wholeness in her family and community, because she lives a life of grace. Her life of thanksgiving would be very familiar to Chesterton who, as we have seen, tried to live each day with child-like wonder and thankfulness. As we saw earlier, after reading Chesterton and MacDonald, Lewis likewise saw particularities in the world as imbued with grace—sacraments for which to be thankful.

22. Lewis, *Till*, 305.
23. Ibid., 308.
24. Berry, *Hannah*, 5.

Finally, let us return to our initial question, "What are humans for?" In chapter 3 we discussed how "humans should be valued because they are humans."[25] In other words, they are to be valued in themselves. As we have seen, the writings of Chesterton, Lewis, and Berry invite us to value ourselves and each other because we owe our very existence to grace—we did not speak ourselves into being. Their writings, therefore, are a valuable inclusion in a humanities curriculum, as they help interrupt the patterns of objectification and instrumentalism with which we, as moderns, are so used to thinking.

25. See page 76.

BIBLIOGRAPHY

Arendt, Hannah. *The Human Condition*. 2nd ed. Chicago: Chicago University Press, 1998.
Aristotle. *The Nicomachean Ethics*. Translated by David Ross. Oxford: Oxford University Press, 2009.
———. *Politics*. Translated by B. Jowett. In vol. 2 of *Complete Works of Aristotle: The Revised Oxford Translation*. Edited by Jonathan Barnes. 2 vols. Bollingen Series. Princeton: Princeton University Press, 1983.
Belloc, Hilaire. *The Servile State*. 3rd ed. London: Constable, 1927.
Benson, Iain T. "Introduction." In *The Collected Works of G. K. Chesterton*, vol. 7, 15–32. San Francisco: Ignatius, 2004.
Benson, Robert. "Curing Babylon." *Sewanee Review* 116 (2008) 274–83.
Berger, Rose Marie. "Heaven in Henry County: A *Sojourners* Interview with Wendell Berry." 2004. In *Conversations with Wendell Berry*, edited by Morris Allen Grubbs, 164–77. Jackson: University Press of Mississippi, 2007.
Berry, Wendell. "An Argument for Diversity." 1988. In *What Matters?: Economics for a Renewed Commonwealth*, 75–88. Berkeley: Counterpoint, 2010.
———. "Conservation Is Good Work." 1991. In *Sex, Economy, Freedom & Community: Eight Essays*, 27–43. New York: Pantheon, 1993.
———. "Fidelity." 1992. In *That Distant Land: The Collected Stories*, 372–427. Washington, DC: Shoemaker, 2004.
———. "The Gift of Gravity." In *The Selected Poems of Wendell Berry*, 139–40. New York: Counterpoint, 1998.
———. *Hannah Coulter: A Novel*. Washington, DC: Shoemaker, 2004.
———. *Jayber Crow*. Washington, DC: Counterpoint, 2000.
———. *The Long-Legged House*. 1969. Washington, DC: Shoemaker, 2004.
———. *The Memory of Old Jack*. 1974. Berkeley: Counterpoint, 1999. Kindle edition.
———. "Money Versus Goods." 2009. In *What Matters?: Economics for a Renewed Commonwealth*, 3–30. Berkeley: Counterpoint, 2010.
———. "A Nation Rich in Natural Resources." 1985. In *What Matters?: Economics for a Renewed Commonwealth*, 71–74. Berkeley: Counterpoint, 2010.
———. "The Peace of Wild Things." In *The Selected Poems of Wendell Berry*, 30. New York: Counterpoint, 1998.
———. "Poetry and Place." 1982. In *Standing by Words*, 106–213. Washington, DC: Shoemaker, 2005.

———. *Remembering*. 1988. In *Three Short Novels*, 119–222. Washington, DC: Counterpoint, 2002.

———. "Simple Solutions, Package Deals, and a 50-Year Farm Bill." 2009. In *What Matters?: Economics for a Renewed Commonwealth*, 55–67. Berkeley: Counterpoint, 2010.

———. "The Total Economy." 2000. In *What Matters?: Economics for a Renewed Commonwealth*, 177–93. Berkeley: Counterpoint, 2010.

———. "Two Economies." 1988. In *What Matters?: Economics for a Renewed Commonwealth*, 115–37. Berkeley: Counterpoint, 2010.

———. *The Unsettling of America: Culture & Agriculture*. New York: Avon, 1977.

———. "What Are People For?" 1985. In *What Matters?: Economics for a Renewed Commonwealth*, 105–7. Berkeley: Counterpoint, 2010.

Bilbro, Jeffrey. "Phantastical Regress: The Return of Desire and Deed in *Phantastes* and *The Pilgrim's Regress*." *Mythlore* 109/110 (2010) 21–37.

Bouma-Prediger, Steven. *For the Beauty of the Earth: A Christian Vision for Creation Care*. 2nd ed. Grand Rapids: Baker Academic, 2010.

Bryson, J. Scott. *The West Side of Any Mountain: Place, Space, and Ecopoetry*. Iowa City: University of Iowa Press, 2005.

Burleigh, Anne Husted. "Wendell Berry's Community." 2000. In *Conversations with Wendell Berry*, edited by Morris Allen Grubbs, 135–46. Jackson: University Press of Mississippi, 2007.

Carlson, Allan. "Wendell Berry and the Twentieth-Century Agrarian 'Series.'" In *Wendell Berry: Life and Work*, edited by Jason Peters, 96–111. Lexington: University Press of Kentucky, 2007.

Carretero-González, Margarita. "Sons of Adam, Daughters of Eve, and Children of Aslan: An Environmentalist Perspective on *The Chronicles of Narnia*." In vol. 2 of *C. S. Lewis: Life, Works, and Legacy*, edited by Bruce L. Edwards, 93–113. Westport, CT: Praeger, 2007.

Chesterton, G. K. *The Autobiography of G. K. Chesterton*. 1936. San Francisco: Ignatius, 2006.

———. *The Defendant*. New York: Dodd, 1902.

———. *The Everlasting Man*. 1925. San Francisco: Ignatius, 1993.

———. *The Flying Inn*. 1914. Reprinted in *The Collected Works of G. K. Chesterton*, vol. 7, 421–665. San Francisco: Ignatius, 2004.

———. *Heretics*. 1905. New York: Barnes & Noble, 2007.

———. *Manalive*. 1912. Reprinted in *The Collected Works of G. K. Chesterton*, vol. 7, 259–419. San Francisco: Ignatius, 2004.

———. *The Man Who Was Thursday*. 1908. Reprinted, London: Penguin, 1986.

———. *The Napoleon of Notting Hill*. 1904. Reprinted, New York: Dover, 1991.

———. *Orthodoxy*. 1908. Reprinted, Colorado Springs: WaterBrook, 2001.

———. *The Outline of Sanity*. New York: Dodd, 1927.

———. "The Patriotic Idea." *The Chesterton Review* 30 (2004) 225–45.

———. "The Queer Feet." *The Complete Father Brown*, 39–53. London: Penguin, 1981.

———. *A Short History of England*. 1917. Available on Project Gutenberg, 2013. http://www.gutenberg.org/ebooks/20897/.

———. *What's Wrong with the World*. 1910. San Francisco: Ignatius, 1994.

———. *Wine, Water, and Song*. London: Methuen, 1915.

BIBLIOGRAPHY

Christian Century. "Toward a Healthy Community: An Interview with Wendell Berry." 1997. Reprinted in *Conversations with Wendell Berry,* edited by Morris Allen Grubbs, 164–77. Jackson: University Press of Mississippi, 2007.

Cloutier, David. "Working with the Grammar of Creation: Benedict XVI, Wendell Berry, and the Unity of the Catholic Moral Vision." *Communio* 37 (2010) 606–33.

Deneen, Patrick J. "Wendell Berry and the Alternative Tradition in American Political Thought." In *Wendell Berry: Life and Work,* edited by Jason Peters, 300–15. Lexington: University Press of Kentucky, 2007.

Dickerson, Matthew and David O'Hara. *Narnia and the Fields of Arbol: The Environmental Vision of C. S. Lewis.* Lexington: University Press of Kentucky, 2009.

Dreyfus, Hubert and Sean Dorrance Kelly. *All Things Shining: Reading the Western Classics to Find Meaning in a Secular Age.* New York: Free, 2011.

Eliot, T. S. *Collected Poems: 1909–1962.* New York: Harcourt, 1963.

Fitzgerald, F. Scott. "Letter to Max Perkins, May 1, 1925." In *The Sons of Maxwell Perkins: Letters of F. Scott Fitzgerald, Ernest Hemingway, Thomas Wolfe, and Their Editor,* edited by Matthew Bruccoli with Judith Baughman, 46–48. Columbia: University of South Carolina, 2004.

Friedman, Thomas L. "Made in the World." *New York Times,* January 29, 2012.

Gardner, Martin. Introduction to *The Napoleon of Notting Hill,* by G. K. Chesterton, vii–xx. New York: Dover, 1991.

Goethe, Johann Wolfgang von. "Nature and art." In *Selected Poetry,* translated by David Luke, 125–26. London: Penguin, 1999/2005.

Gresham, Douglas. "Interview with Max McLean." *The Christian Post,* June 17, 2010. http://christianpost.tv/interview-with-max-mclean-and-douglas-gresham-son-of-c-s-lewis-1826/.

Grubbs, Morris Allen, ed. *Conversations with Wendell Berry.* Jackson: University Press of Mississippi, 2007.

The Holy Bible, English Standard Version. Wheaton, IL: Good News, 2007.

King James Version. http://biblegateway.com/.

Kraybill, Donald. "Introduction: The Struggle to Be Separate." In *The Amish Struggle with Modernity,* edited by Donald Kraybill and Marc Olshan, 1–17. Hanover: University Press of New England, 1994.

Kraybill, Donald, and Marc Olshan. "Editors' Preface." In *The Amish Struggle with Modernity,* edited by Donald Kraybill and Marc Olshan, vii–ix. Hanover: University Press of New England, 1994.

Kroeker, Travis P. "Sexuality and the Sacramental Imagination: It All Turns on Affection." In *Wendell Berry: Life and Work,* edited by Jason Peters, 119–36. Lexington: University Press of Kentucky, 2007.

Levertov, Denise. "Tragic Error." In *Evening Train,* 69. New York: New Directions, 1992.

Lewis, C. S. *The Abolition of Man.* 1944. Reprinted, San Francisco: Harper, 2001.

———. *The Collected Letters of C. S. Lewis: Family Letters 1905–1931,* Vol. 1 of *The Collected Letters of C. S. Lewis,* edited by Walter Hooper. 3 vols. San Francisco: Harper-SanFrancisco, 2004.

———. *The Four Loves.* New York: Harcourt Brace, 1960.

———. *The Horse and His Boy.* 1954. Reprinted, New York: Scholastic, 1988.

———. *Letters to Malcolm: Chiefly on Prayer.* New York: Harcourt, 1963, 1964.

———. *The Lion, the Witch and the Wardrobe.* 1950. Reprinted, New York: Scholastic, 1987.

———. *The Magician's Nephew*. 1955. Reprinted, New York: Scholastic, 1988.

———. *Out of the Silent Planet*. 1938. Reprinted, New York: Scribner, 1996.

———. "The Pains of Animals: A Problem in Theology." Reprinted in *The Timeless Writings of C. S. Lewis*, 408–15. New York: Inspirational, 1996.

———. *Perelandra*. 1944. Reprinted, New York: Scribner, 1996.

———. *The Pilgrim's Regress*. 1933. Reprinted in *The Timeless Writings of C. S. Lewis*, 1–161. New York: Inspirational, 1996.

———. *The Problem of Pain*. New York: Macmillan, 1944.

———. *Surprised by Joy: The Shape of My Early Life*. New York: Harcourt, 1955.

———. *That Hideous Strength: A Modern Fairy-Tale for Grown-Ups*. 1945. Reprinted, New York: Scribner, 1996.

———. *Till We Have Faces: A Myth Retold*. 1956. Reprinted, New York: Harvest, 1984.

———. "Vivisection." In *The Timeless Writings of C. S. Lewis*, 451–54. New York: Inspirational, 1996.

MacIntyre, Alasdair. *After Virtue: A Study in Moral Theory*. 2nd ed. Notre Dame: University of Notre Dame Press, 1984.

McNabb, Fr. Vincent. *The Church and the Land*. 1925. Reprinted, Norfolk, VA: IHS, 2003. E-book.

Minick, Jim. "A Citizen and a Native: An Interview with Wendell Berry." 2004. In *Conversations with Wendell Berry*, edited by Morris Allen Grubbs, 147–63. Jackson: University Press of Mississippi, 2007.

Murdoch, Iris. *The Sovereignty of Good*. 1970. Reprinted, New York: Routledge, 2009.

Naylor, Thomas H. "Averting Self-Destruction: A Twenty-First Century Appraisal of Distributism." In *Distributist Perspectives: Volume 1*. Norfolk, VA: IHS, 2004. E-book.

Oddie, William. *Chesterton and the Romance of Orthodoxy: The Making of GKC 1874–1908*. Oxford: Oxford University Press, 2008.

Pennington, Vince. "Interview with Wendell Berry." 1991/1996. In *Conversations with Wendell Berry*, edited by Morris Allen Grubbs, 36–49. Jackson: University Press of Mississippi, 2007.

Penty, Arthur J. "Distributism: A Manifesto." 1937. Reprinted, in *Distributist Perspectives: Volume 1*. Norfolk, VA: IHS, 2004. E-book.

Peters, Jason. "Education, Heresy, and the 'Deadly Disease of the World.'" In *Wendell Berry: Life and Work*, edited by Jason Peters, 256–81. Lexington: University Press of Kentucky, 2007.

Rerum Novarum, Encyclical of Pope Leo XIII on Capital and Labor. Vatican City: Libreria Editrice Vaticana, 1891. http://w2.vatican.va/content/leo-xiii/en/encyclicals/documents/hf_l-xiii_enc_15051891_rerum-novarum.html/.

Sayer, George. *Jack: A Life of C. S. Lewis*. 2nd ed. Wheaton, IL: Crossway, 1994. Nook book.

Schlueter, Nathan. "Healing the Hidden Wound: The Theology of the Body in Wendell Berry's *Remembering*." *Communio* 36 (2009) 510–33.

Shiffman, Mark. "An Ethic of Attentiveness: The Rediscovery of Oikonomia." *Communio* 36 (2009) 487–509.

Shuman, Joel, and L. Roger Owens, eds. *Wendell Berry and Religion: Heaven's Earthly Life*. Lexington: University Press of Kentucky, 2009.

Smith, Jordan Fisher. "Field Observations: An Interview with Wendell Berry." 1993. In *Conversations with Wendell Berry*, edited by Morris Allen Grubbs, 86–102. Jackson: University Press of Mississippi, 2007.

Steiner, George. *Real Presences*. Chicago: University of Chicago Press, 1989.
Taylor, Charles. *Philosophical Arguments*. Cambridge: Harvard University Press, 1995.
———. *Sources of the Self: The Making of the Modern Identity*. Cambridge: Harvard University Press, 1989.
Teachout, Terry. "A Twitch Upon the Thread." *National Review* 34.19 (1982) 1230–31.
Tolkien, J. R. R. *The Fellowship of the Ring*. 1954. Reprinted, Boston: Houghton Mifflin, 1994.
Ward, Maisie. *Gilbert Keith Chesterton*. New York: Sheed, 1943.
Waugh, Evelyn. *Brideshead Revisited*. 1945. Reprinted, New York: Everyman's Library, 1993.
Wetmore, Jameson. "Amish Technology: Reinforcing Values and Building Community." In *Technology and Society: Building Our Sociotechnical Future*, edited by Deborah Johnson and Jameson Wetmore, 297–318. Cambridge: MIT Press, 2009.
Wheat, Andrew. "The Road Before Him: Allegory, Reason, And Romanticism in C. S. Lewis' *The Pilgrim's Regress*." *Renascence* 51.1 (1998) 21–39.
White, Lynn, Jr. "The Historical Roots of Our Ecological Crisis." *Science*, n.s. 155/3767 (1967) 1203–7.
The Who. "The Seeker," by Pete Townsend, Decca, recorded 1970. MCA Records 088 112 877-2, 2002, compact disc.
Young, R. V. "Harold Bloom: The Critic as Gnostic." *Modern Age* 47.1 (2005) 19–29.

NAME/SUBJECT INDEX

agrarian, 65, 70, 90
Amish, 17, 57–60, 67, 97
Arendt, Hannah, 3n11, 3n13, 18n35,
    36–37, 39, 48, 58–59, 63, 96,
    100, 119–20
Aristotle, 1–2, 7, 16–17, 34n116,
    48–50, 53n33, 62–63, 66, 68,
    75, 100

Belloc, Hilaire, 64, 69
Benson, Iain T., 34
Benson, Robert, 6–8
Berger, Rose Marie, 70n115
Berry, Wendell
    "Fidelity," 42, 111–13
    "The Gift of Gravity," 130
    Great Economy, 48, 96–97
    Hannah Coulter, 107, 133
    Jayber Crow, 33, 41–45, 107, 109
    The Memory of Old Jack, 109–11
    "The Peace of Wild Things," 130
    Remembering, 7, 59–61, 97–98,
        109, 116–17
    *The Unsettling of America: Culture
        and Agriculture*, 67n90, 95,
        101, 103n14, 108n34, 120–21
Bilbro, Jeffrey, 37–38
Bloom, Harold, 87n40
Bouma-Prediger, Steven, 94n75
Bryson, J. Scott, 99–100, 104, 119
Burleigh, Anne Husted, 46, 48, 65n82

Carlson, Allan, 5–6
Carretero-González, Margarita, 91
Catholic(ism), Roman, 5–8n29,
    15n16, 23, 30n98, 54, 64, 66,
    100, 105n27, 127n2, 132
Chesterton, G. K.
    The Flying Inn, 53, 77–80, 105–6
    Heretics, 14–19, 30n95, 32n111
    Manalive, 20, 33–37, 108
    The Man Who Was Thursday,
        113–15
    The Napoleon of Notting Hill,
        77–78
    Orthodoxy, 7, 12, 14, 19–20, 26,
        35–36, 50–51, 79n21, 101–2,
        108, 113–14, 118, 122,
Christ(ic), 6–8, 87, 98n95, 115
Christian Century, 26n71
Cloutier, David, 30n98
colonization, 78n17, 90, 95, 98
communitarian, 17
community, 1, 3–4, 6, 8–10, 12n2, 26,
    42–43, 49–50, 52, 54, 57–60,
    65–70, 72, 75, 83–84, 92n61,
    97, 100–102, 106–8, 113, 115,
    117, 120–21, 123–24, 131,
    133
consumer(ism), 1, 32, 58, 65, 68, 120,
    133
consumption, 119–120; *see*
    consumer(ism)

NAME/SUBJECT INDEX

Creator, God as, 8, 24, 31, 39, 46, 73, 114
Creed, Apostles', 7–8, 13
culture(less), 2–3, 9–10, 28, 47, 52, 58, 66–67, 70, 78, 84–87, 93, 99–101, 104, 106, 108, 119

Deneen, Patrick J., 94–95
Derrida, Jacques, 12n2, 112n51
Dickerson, Matthew, 70n116, 91
Distributist(s), 6, 64–70, 138
Dreyfus, Hubert, 84n33

ecology, including ecologists, 18, 81, 91
economic(s), including economical, 7, 9, 46–71, 76, 78n17, 92, 94–95, 99–100, 119
Eliot, T. S., 2, 4, 82n28
Enlightenment, the, 2, 4, 8, 15n16, 30, 37, 47, 58, 72, 82, 94
environment, including environmental and environmentalists, 1, 5, 18, 45, 47, 49, 51, 75, 81, 84, 86–87, 91, 96, 123–24
escape
    from the Earth, 3–4, 9, 36–37, 39, 96
    from limiting values, religions, and traditions, 10, 12, 20, 38, 60
    from a place, 29, 61
ethic(s), including ethical, 2n9, 7–10, 15–17, 19, 21, 30n98, 45–71, 73, 75, 77, 81–82, 84, 84n33–34, 87, 91, 93n70, 96n86, 98–102, 104–5, 118, 122
eudaimonia, 49, 53, 61

family, respectful engagement with, 104–7
fidelity, 42, 107–13, 123
fin de siècle, 14, 16, 33
Fitzgerald, F. Scott, 2–3
framework(s), Charles Taylor's "inescapable frameworks," 2–3, 12, 15, 17–18, 20, 45, 56–57, 73, 81, 93, 96, 98, 101
Friedman, Thomas L., 95n83

Gardner, Martin, 77n12
Gnostic(ism), 8, 23, 30n98, 86–87
Goethe, Johann Wolfgang von, 117
good life, 1, 3, 34n116, 56n45, 62, 66, 72, 74–76, 91, 93, 105
grace, including Grace, 31, 127–34
Gresham, Douglas, 129
Grubbs, Morris Allen, 28n82

health, 103–4
    of communities and places, 49, 61, 70, 74–75, 97, 101, 103–4, 107, 113, 115, 117, 121, 123–24, 131, 133; see wholeness
    regarding economics, 69–70
Heaven, 3–4, 7, 30n98, 31, 39n134, 45, 73–74, 86, 130
humanities, 9–10, 13, 33, 45, 47, 50, 52n28, 54n37, 72–73, 83–84, 87, 93, 99, 119, 121–22, 124–25, 131, 134
hypergood(s), 11, 56–57, 81, 101, 104, 106–9, 111, 113, 121–24, 127, 131

imperialism, 9, 72–98
Incarnation(al), 36, 113
individual(ism), 1–2, 10, 17, 47, 58, 72, 74–76, 101, 105, 108, 124, 132
Industrial Revolution, 8, 58, 63, 67
institution(s), 3, 8, 57–58, 91, 98, 100
    the Church or Christianity as an, 5–6, 8–9, 100–101
instrumentalism, 2, 24–25, 47, 75–76, 79, 81, 83, 85, 90–91, 96, 131, 134
interdependence, including interdependent, 33, 74, 99, 104, 121

Kelly, Sean Dorrance, 84n33

NAME/SUBJECT INDEX

Kingdom of God, 5, 39, 48, 96; *see* Berry, Great Economy
Kraybill, Donald, 57–58
Kroeker, Travis P., 5–6

Levertov, Denise, 94
Lewis, C. S.
   The Abolition of Man, 55–57, 84n34, 86, 101–3, 106, 116
   The Four Loves, 129
   The Horse and His Boy, 116
   joy, 20–23, 31, 39, 39n134
   Letters to Malcolm, 39n134
   The Lion, the Witch, and the Wardrobe, 21, 66, 107
   The Magician's Nephew, 66, 87–91
   Out of the Silent Planet, 55, 66n85, 83, 84n34, 115
   Perelandra, 55, 83, 109, 115, 118–19
   The Pilgrim's Regress, 21, 33, 37–41, 55
   The Problem of Pain, 87n42
   Surprised by Joy, 20–25, 53–54
   That Hideous Strength, 55, 83, 85–86, 95, 108
   Till We Have Faces, 132–33

MacDonald, George, 18, 23–24, 37–38, 82, 133
MacIntyre, Alasdair, 2, 15n16, 16n22, 17, 48–49, 79–80, 82, 100, 105, 117
magician, 22, 56–57, 66, 87–90
marriage, 27–28, 34n116, 42, 106, 108–9, 111, 124, 133
McNabb, Fr. Vincent, 64, 67–69
Minick, Jim, 70n113
morality, 14–16, 56, 82, 86, 102n12
Murdoch, Iris, 73n2

Naylor, Thomas H., 64n77

Oddie, William, 12n4, 14n11, 14n15, 115n60, 128
O'Hara, David, 70n116, 91
oikonomia, 62

orthodox(y), including Orthodox(y), 3–15, 8n29, 18–23, 25, 30n98, 34, 51, 53, 57, 65n80, 86, 100–102, 108, 113, 124; *see* Chesterton, *Orthodoxy*

paradox(ical), 18, 47, 113, 117–18, 123
Pater, Walter, 14, 14n13,
patriotism, 50–52
Pennington, Vince, 49n15
Penty, Arthur J., 64–68
Peters, Jason, 30n98, 86
postmodern, including postmodernism, 12n2, 87n40, 112n51
progress, as a philosophy of modern life, 11–12, 15–18, 51, 53, 57–58, 66, 75–76, 80, 82–83, 86, 89, 95–96, 117, 122

Reformation, Protestant, 3, 72, 74n7, 100–101
Rerum Novarum, 64

Sabbath, 8, 98
sacrament(al) imagination, 5–6, 10, 23–25, 31, 39, 46, 74n7, 75, 104, 133
Sayer, George, 20n42, 20n44, 22n52, 23n59, 25n69, 55n42
Schlueter, Nathan, 7
science, 9, 13, 15, 18n32, 47, 72, 93
scientist, 56, 75, 83, 87, 90, 92
Sen, Amartya, 49n17
sex(uality), 7, 34n116, 110, 112, 118
Shiffman, Mark, 7
Smith, Jordan Fisher, 49n16, 51n26
socialism, 64
specialization, 9, 96, 121
Steiner, George, 80n24
steward(ship), 37–38, 46, 48, 74n7, 75, 87, 90, 93

Taylor, Charles, 1–3, 11–12, 16–18, 30, 34, 47–52, 54–56, 72–74, 82m 87m 93m 96m 100, 103–4, 109, 112, 139

NAME/SUBJECT INDEX

teaching, 7, 28, 30, 50, 124
Teachout, Terry, 132
technocrat(ic), 53, 79, 80, 85, 95, 105
technology, 18n32, 19, 31–32, 43, 57–61, 66–67, 100, 104, 120
teleology, 12, 16n22, 36, 52–53, 82–83
telos, also teloi, 1, 15n16, 17, 34, 39, 48–49, 52, 54, 57, 63, 73–74, 93, 97, 124
Tolkien, J. R. R., 116n65
transcendence, including Transcendence, 36, 104, 113, 115–16, 122–24
Turner, Kate, 70n116

usury, 63–64, 68, 70, 70n117
utilitarianism, 10, 29, 46, 53, 66, 72, 75–76, 79, 82, 87, 108, 131

Ward, Maisie, 13n5
Waugh, Evelyn, 132
Wetmore, Jameson, 58
Wheat, Andrew, 38
White, Lynn, Jr., 94n75
The Who, 2n9
wholeness, as a measure for health, 11, 12n2, 99–125, 131, 133
Wilson, E. O., 102n12

Young, R. V., 87n40

SCRIPTURE INDEX

OLD TESTAMENT

Genesis
1:28	94
1:31	73

Psalms
65:9–13	127

Isaiah
58:6–7	128
65:17–25	73

NEW TESTAMENT

Revelation
21:1–5	74